The Second Amendment and Hunting Heritage

By Charlie Kirk

Published by
the Conklin Endowment Fund

Providing Our Nation's Youth
with Needed Facts By a
20-Year-Old Author

W9-CHX-581

Contents

Foreword I

T his book and all rights are the property of the Conklin Endowment Fund and the Conklin Foundation.

The Conklin Foundation is a hunting organization sponsoring a hunting award each year to a serious hunter who not only has to be ethical but also a conservationist. The Conklin Endowment Fund is a sister organization which raises money every year and distributes it to conservation efforts.

The purpose of the Conklin organizations to own this book is to distribute it to youth groups all across the country and to make it available for purchase so young people are aware of our hunting heritage and facts and necessary information about the Second Amendment.

Foreword II

Growing up in a non-hunting family and in an area that did not have a gun ownership cornerstone to everyday living, I was educated and raised in a community that perpetuated and advanced false narratives about hunting and the Second Amendment. Throughout my upbringing I had an inherent fear of guns. My teachers told me they were evil and dangerous, and most of my friends, including me, believed they were. Not until I met Mike Miller and other hunters from across the country in my political travels did I begin to change my viewpoint on guns. I realized that guns are merely tools, a means to an end. My old preconceived notions that hunters want to kill everything in sight were shattered by the gentle, loving, conservation-minded spirit of hunters. I then realized our school system and learning institutions had put my thought process on a path against gun ownership and hunting. If it were not for these mentors and individuals, I would have never been able to go pheasant hunting or shoot trap and skeet.

When I was approached by Tom Hammond from the Conklin Foundation to write a book designed for young people, I was immediately enthusiastic in agreeing to do so. For a long while before that, I was waiting for a way to combat the falsehoods regarding hunting and the Second Amendment advanced in our high schools and colleges, but I was unsure about what was the best way to do so. This book gives me the unique opportunity to arm our youth with the facts, statistics, stories, and principled values to defend gun ownership and hunting. Myths in this book are what I have heard and been taught by people in academia.

Remember, when you read this book, turn the information into real-life debates and rebuttals. I am confident that at the completion of reading this book, no teacher, professor, or friend would be able to attack hunting or gun ownership with any substantive backing. It is our duty to stand up for what we believe in and defend the ideals that have made this country the greatest in the world.

I just turned 20 years old. The information I am providing you was provided to me. I made up my own mind. I challenge you, boy or girl, to make up your own mind. You have to believe in the Second Amendment, or we, our generation, could see in our lifetimes a threat to our freedom as we know it. Hunting, hopefully you will see, is more than just killing—it is a recreation that many hunters turn into conservation.

Information used in this book is all general information, to my knowledge, and not from a specific source, with the exception of our Constitution.

Charles Kirk

Introduction

As told by Michael J. Miller

It was a regular mid-November day, just like any other. I woke up at 4:30 a.m., well before the crack of dawn. I rolled out of bed; slipped on my boots, which were still muddy from the previous day; rubbed the sleep out of my eyes; and made my way to the door. My dad was already awake and was returning from the barn.

We both knew the drill by then. I loaded up the pickup with enough shells, my dad filled the thermos with hot chocolate, and I double-checked all the details, making sure we had plenty of gas to make it to the lake. Dad took a little longer than usual, so I used the extra five minutes to double-check my shell supply and tie my boots. Just the thought of hunting woke me up like a shot of adrenaline.

Looking at my Winchester Model 12, with the bluing worn down, an unusual sense of nostalgia hit me. I began to think of my childhood. I had an unusual upbringing. My first job, at the age of five, was the "gunner" at the local slaughterhouse. That was my job, and boy I did it well.

At age 11, Dad came to me and said, "Your mother and I haven't had a trip since our honeymoon, which was two weeks before I went to Guadalcanal for two years. We need to get away. I know you can drive well, handle the store, and outshoot anyone in town, so here, Michael, are the keys to the truck and the keys to the store and to my 1911 Colt 45. Doors open at 6 a.m. and close at 10 p.m. Look after the store. There will be a pharmacist for eight hours a day. Keep an eye on him as well. We will be back in two weeks." And that was the drill. That was life, living in North Dakota.

In those days we got our driver's learning permits at nine and our driver's licenses at 10. There was no *Sesame Street* or Legos. One grew up in a hurry. Kids walked to school with shotguns over their shoulders, and they kept them in their school lockers during the day. It was nothing out of the ordinary. Everybody hunted on the way to school and on the way home. Every week, after school, we got an hour of gun safety and conservation education with the old game warden. I never looked at my gun as a weapon but rather as a tool necessary for survival. It was part of my life and my upbringing.

"OK, time to go," Dad said as he threw himself into the pickup. He started the engine, and we were off. Just like any hunting duo, we had our favorite spots. We both knew where the geese liked to fly in the morning, and we knew exactly where to hide. As our '60 Chevy pickup roared down the road, I became excited even more, for I knew I was one step closer to a great morning of hunting.

My dad and I were so close that we discussed almost everything in life and picked each other's brains. He was a man of few words, but the words he chose I thought were from God. He was my hero then and still is to this day. He served in World War II and fought in Guadalcanal. After a short stint in New York, he ventured back to North Dakota to raise me and my siblings.

At the age of 42 he saw the need to receive a formal education as a pharmacist, even though at this point he owned a drug, jewelry, and gun store—all under the same roof. Rising at 4 a.m. daily, he went to the store to repair watches and open up the store. The part-time pharmacist would arrive at 6 a.m., and Dad would get to school just in time for his first class at 8 a.m. He packed all of his courses into three days per week and got back home to close the store at the end of the day. He would do his homework, repair more watches, and still manage to snag a few hours of sleep. Dad did all of this while pulling straight A's throughout college.

When it came time for graduation, we were not surprised that my dad was valedictorian, which he accomplished while raising a family and running a business. During the day, Dad was a chain-smoker and ate like a wild horse, and right before bed every night, he would eat half a gallon of ice cream. He never put on one pound. Some people are just born greater than others, I suppose.

Dad felt emotions deeply, but he did not wear his emotions on his sleeve. People of that generation taught themselves to internalize almost everything.

He saw things, terrible things, in the war that I never want to think of. Dad always told me, "Mike, you can ask me about anything, but just don't ask me about the war," and I always respected that. He was the toughest man I knew. Whatever emotion he showed, no matter how sad or angry he got, it was always brewing on the inside.

We pulled up to the big rock pile on the south side of Lake Alice on Mr. Nottlemeyer's property, grabbed our gear, and walked down to our favorite goose pits. I was unsure why I was having such feelings of nostalgia during this particular hunt. Not thinking too much of it, I loaded my gun and began to look for geese as they started to cross overhead.

As dawn began to break, the snow drove out of the north and the temperature fell; it was apparent that this was going to be the last day of the season for the waterfowl.

We both waited patiently as the birds began to move in the distance. Having used this Model 12 since I was a young boy, now at 18, I could not estimate how many rounds I had shot in that gun. It was an extension of my arm.

I was sitting there in a blind; I was ready to shoot and looked up as the geese began to get close. We took the proper lead, having to judge the correct speed and wind velocity to get a perfect shot. Having shot all types of birds and big game all over the world, I must say a wonderful goose shoot and taking down a magnificent Cape buffalo are two of the most exciting ways to spend a morning hunting, especially with your dad.

As the shooting intensified, I started to reflect on the next couple of months. I was going to college, and I was going to leave home for the first time in my life.

I loved diamonds, and I really wanted to get into that business. I loved diamonds since the first time I laid my eyes on them. I remember when my dad introduced me to some basic pearls and shiny objects. I immediately fell in love. I knew that it was what I wanted to do for the rest of my life. My parents understood my love for gems and precious jewels, but they wanted me to get a college degree in something—to get a formal education to round out my life.

I applied and got accepted into the pharmacy program at North Dakota State University. Half of me was nervous, and the other was excited. I would sure miss hunting with my dad; we did it almost every day. It became a family tradition of sorts. But I knew I needed to move on with my formal education, one of the definite requests of my parents.

After a good hour of shooting we collected our legal limit of birds and called it a morning. I cleaned the guns, took a swig of water, and loaded everything back into the pickup. Nothing was out of the ordinary about that day, but it was one I would remember for the rest of my life.

Dad finished cleaning up the birds, threw them in the back of the pickup truck, and we headed home. By that time it was late morning, and the storm had begun to pick up. Dad was not very talkative, which was not unusual after a hunt. I peered out my window at the rolling farm country and the endless plains that hit the sky. I thought about pharmacy school, I thought about diamonds, I thought about living in a big city, I thought about almost everything while riding through the country. I got this eerie feeling as I yawned and tried to start a conversation with Dad.

I saw tears flowing down his face, and I asked, "Dad, are you all right?"

He looked at me, and barely able to say the words, he said, "After today, I just realized, with you going to college and leaving the house, I am going to lose my hunting buddy."

Myth: The Majority of Americans Favor New Gun Control

I t is important to remember that, anytime you are talking about polls or public opinion, you must take into account how the question is being asked and who is asking the question. Polls can be swayed to get almost any result if the pollster leads the person being questioned or strongly slants words in a way to get her or him to answer a certain way.

When talking about gun control and how it relates to public opinion, we must first understand that the majority of Americans do not understand, or perhaps don't even know about, the gun laws that are currently in place. When these "flash polls" come out from the media saying that "68% of Americans favor more gun control," we must first pick apart the exact way the question was asked and look at other external factors that may have played into the current mindset.

Shortly after the Newtown tragedy, public support for more gun control saw a small spike in polling. Historically, polls show trends in favor of gun control go up after gun-related tragedies, such as after Columbine, Virginia Tech, and Sandy Hook. Looking at a sampling of one static period of time can be extremely deceiving, for it is not the aggregate belief of the population that is being represented. Essentially, public opinion on gun control sees spikes when tragedies occur, but over longer periods of time, Americans consistently support the Second Amendment and are against gun control measures.

If you look at CBS polling taken after the Sandy Hook shooting, support for more gun control went up to 57%. Just three months later, in March, public opinion for gun control went down to 47%, indicating that less than a majority of Americans supported the measures. The number continually dropped into the lower 40th percentile, where it flatlined in the months that followed.

Also, when polling is taken, we must analyze where the callers are being sampled from. Most reputable polling agencies, such as Gallup or Rasmussen, do a reasonable job of spreading out national polls to various demographics and regions across the country. Unfortunately, this is not always the case with polling done by media organizations.

For example, if the majority of the polling was taken in areas with high levels of gun crime, such as on the South Side of Chicago or in Detroit, the respondents would be more likely to favor increased gun control. But if the respondents were from Wyoming or Montana, they would most likely oppose additional measures because their state crime rates are extremely low. When polling is done, it is important to take into account exactly who is answering the question and whether the results of the poll are an accurate snapshot of how Americans stand on an issue.

Finally, as mentioned above, much of the time when polling is done, the people being polled do not have the entire knowledge or understanding of what is being asked. This is done intentionally to try to sway the results.

A good example would be in April 2013, when President Obama stated, "Find out where your member of Congress stands on this. If they're not part of the 90% of Americans who agree on background checks, then ask them, why not?" He used a variety of polls from the media to say that 90% of Americans support background checks.

The people being polled at that time most likely did not know the following regarding "background checks" nor did they know anything about the background check bill that was being proposed in the Senate:

- The bill in the Senate would require a background check for borrowing a friend's hunting rifle, and failure to do so would be a felony.
- The bill in the Senate would weaken mental health privacy laws, specifically in the Schumer-Toomey-Manchin Amendment. It stated

the bill would "reduce existing privacy protection for mental health relevant to background checks."

- The bill in the Senate would require a background check costing up to $125, according to the Schumer-Toomey-Manchin Amendment.

Chances are that most of the people being polled were not aware of these provisions in the bill. Therefore, it is safe to assume that 90% of Americans most likely did not support universal background checks, as the president said.

When dealing with massive polling and the media, especially with the Second Amendment, be careful and analyze exactly who was polled and what was asked, and take into account the temperature of the country when the polling was finished.

Key Points

- Different regions of the country have varying perspectives about gun control; therefore, polling just one region is misleading.

- After tragedies, public support temporarily goes up in favor of more gun laws but then quickly falls back to previous levels.

- Most people being polled usually do not understand the bills that are being discussed, and there are usually provisions in the proposed laws they have never even heard of.

- You need to know the exact question in a poll and exactly what caused the specific question to be asked.

Links

http://heritageaction.com/2013/04/untangling-the-spin-polling-on-background-checks-highly-misleading/

http://www.nationaljournal.com/domesticpolicy/how-democrats-got-gun-control-polling-wrong-20130321

Myth: AR-15s Are "Weapons of War" and Don't Serve a Purpose

This myth is spread mostly because of lack of education regarding guns in general and also because people believe the AR-15 "looks scary." Hollywood movies and theatrical tactics put forward by the media feed this myth continually. The public is made to believe that the AR-15 is a fully automatic weapon that is used only in war. In fact, the opposite is true.

The unique utility and design of the AR-15 type gun is one of the reasons it has become so popular. These guns are used privately for target shooting and hunting small game, as well as for self-defense. In many situations, responsible gun owners turn to an AR-15 type gun for self-protection and the safety of their families, property, and places of business.

A good example of a practical use of the AR-15 in terms of self-defense is the riots in Los Angeles in 1992. In late April 1992 there were six days of rioting throughout Los Angeles. For the most part the police were absent because it was "too dangerous" for them to be out on the streets protecting citizens and enforcing the law.

Overall, 53 people were killed during the rioting, with well over 2,000 people injured. During the riots, shopkeepers and business owners were forced to turn to their own means to defend themselves against the rioters. Certain South Korean business owners who used AR-15s to defend themselves and their places of business were very successful in fending off the looters.

Shopkeepers without AR-15s or other firearms were unable to defend their stores and became the victims of massive looting and rioting.

The AR-15 offered business owners versatility and accuracy that other firearms were not able to offer. Because of the bigger magazine (30 rounds), the shopkeepers easily defended their stores without having to worry about reloading.

The AR-15 gets put in the public consciousness almost every time there is a massive shooting. After the Newtown tragedy, the AR-15 became the target of some members of the media, such as Piers Morgan, and legislators, such as Diane Feinstein from California.

Stephen Halbrook, a constitutional lawyer from Virginia, said, "They get a lot of coverage when there's a tragedy with one, but the number of people unlawfully killed with them is small."

An analysis of why people buy AR-15s shows that most individuals buy them for shooting sports or hunting. According to a survey done by the National Shooting Sports Foundation, "49.1 percent of the AR-15 style rifles they sold were bought for target shooting, up from 46.3% in 2009. Hunting accounted for 22.8% of sales and personal protection was 28.1%."

It's also important to add that there are large groups of women who are extremely vocal in their support of the AR-15. A nationally known conservative activist, Celia Bigelow, wrote a fantastic piece detailing this in the *National Review*. She stated: "Our goal when defending against a home invader is simple: to hit where we aim. One shouldn't underestimate the value of target practice, but using an accurate weapon is the key to hitting a target with ease and confidence." She hit the nail on the head. The AR-15 is one of the few weapons that can offer pinpoint accuracy and the ability to hit your mark almost every time.

Celia continued: "So what's a girl to do? When choosing our tool for home defense, we want the best—in accuracy, handling, and aesthetics. The best choice by all three criteria is—hands down—the AR-15." A person might miss when shooting a handgun, which is usually a close-quarter type weapon. But with 30 rounds, if you keep pulling the trigger, you are bound to hit.

For young women who want to defend themselves, their homes, or their places of business, the AR-15 is a responsible and smart choice. Women who use the AR-15 give positive feedback and say that they "feel more confident" and "hit more targets than ever before." Over and above that, a bad guy might not flinch from one shot, but many shots should turn the tide.

Despite the myths surrounding AR-15s they have many purposes, including hunting, shooting sports, and self-protection. Just because it looks scary does not mean it should be illegal.

With the drug business and the increased aggressive cartel business along our Mexico border, land owners from California to South Texas will be arming themselves more than ever to protect their families and property. The gun of choice will be a reliable and multifiring gun like the AR-15.

Key Points

- During the 1992 Los Angeles riots the AR-15 served as a crucial tool for South Korean shopkeepers in defending their businesses.
- The AR-15 has been the most popular gun for gun owners since 1963 and contributes to only a small percentage of overall gun crime.
- More than three million Americans own an AR-15 type rifle.
- AR-15s offer an easy-to-use gun for young women who want to protect themselves.
- Just because something looks scary does not mean it should be illegal.

Myth: Guns Have Never Prevented a Mass Shooting from Occurring

To address this myth, I will start with a quote from Piers Morgan: "In the last 30 years there have been 62 mass shootings. Not a single one has ever been thwarted by a civilian despite America being a heavily armed country."

First off, this quote is extremely misleading because, of course, none of the mass shootings would have been prevented or else they would not have been able to be called mass shootings. Glenn Beck picked apart this quote from Morgan masterfully by stating, "It's like saying not a single one of the 32,367 traffic fatalities that occurred in 2011 was thwarted by seat belts or air bags or speed limits. Yeah—no kidding, that's why they are fatalities."

There are two fundamental problems with Morgan's argument. The first is that he fails to mention all of the ways guns have prevented massive shootings from occurring in real instances when the perpetrator had intent to kill many people. Also, he fails to mention that many of these shootings happened in gun-free zones or areas in which people were not allowed to be armed or to defend themselves.

To prove this myth wrong, let's look at specific examples of how guns have prevented massive killings from occurring.

December 9, 2007

Colorado Springs, Colorado

On December 9, 2007, Matthew Murray showed up at a Youth with a Mission meeting. After being told he was not allowed to stay the night at the meeting, he opened fire, killing two teenage girls. He managed to escape the incident and traveled south to Colorado Springs.

After arriving and with murderous intent, he emerged from his car and began opening fire on church-goers at the New Life Church. After the shooting in the parking lot, he advanced into the main lobby of the church. It was later found that he said in a blog post, "All I want to do is injure and kill as many of you [Christians] as I can."

Murray might have had his way that day, if it had not been for a brave woman with a gun.

He made his way to the auditorium, when Jeanna Assam, a volunteer security guard, opened fire on him. Using her own concealed pistol, she shot Murray several times until he fell to the ground. Severely injured, he put a pistol to his head and ended his own life.

According to Pastor Boyd of the New Life Church, "She probably saved over 100 lives that day."

When reflecting back on this story, it is disappointing that members of the media, such as Piers Morgan, fail to mention these stories of everyday citizens saving lives and preventing mass shootings from occurring.

October 1, 1997

Pearl, Mississippi

Luke Woodham, a teenager from Pearl, Mississippi, began a murderous campaign when he stabbed and bludgeoned his mother to death. He then stole his mother's car and drove to Pearl High School.

Wearing a trench coat, he entered the school with a rifle hidden from sight and proceeded to shoot two students, one of whom was his former girlfriend. In addition Luke wounded seven other students.

He then left the school, with the intent of going to the local junior high school to continue his line of killings.

When he was in the parking lot, the school's assistant principal retrieved a .45 caliber semiautomatic pistol from his truck and shouted for him to stop.

Woodham ignored his yelling and tried to get away. The assistant principal approached the car and pointed the .45 caliber at Woodham through the windshield. Shocked, Woodham crashed into a pole and laid there until authorities arrived.

It is impossible to know how many lives were saved that day. Police reports later show that more than 30 rounds were found in Luke's pockets when he was officially arrested. A brave man with a gun was able to save many more kids from dying that day.

Nevada, 2008

A man entered a restaurant in Winnemucca, Nevada. He shot two people from a family he was feuding with. Was he going to kill the other patrons in the restaurant? I guess we will never know because another man pulled out his handgun, which was lawfully being carried, pointed the gun at the attacker, and shot him dead.

All of these examples show how guns have prevented terrible mass killings from occurring. As I mentioned before, Morgan fails to mention that many of the recent mass shootings occurred in gun-free zones.

Let's look at the Pearl, Mississippi, incident again. An associate principal was able to stop the shooter from continuing his murderous rampage. It begs the question: What if the principal or security guard had been armed at Sandy Hook or Columbine? Many members on the antigun side try to portray the NRA and advocates of the Second Amendment as "heartless" and "callous" for promoting responsible gun ownership and protection of children in school zones, when in fact, they are looking to history and trying to implement those successes so we don't have any more mass killings.

The solution to ending mass shootings is multifaceted and extremely complex. But it is impossible to ignore true, real-life examples of how guns and responsible gun owners have prevented mass shootings from happening.

About two years ago some states started making it easier and simpler for citizens to have concealed weapons permits. Classes usually were for eight hours to ensure safety and knowledge of the laws. Numerous states have followed through on this, and the states that have this easier concealed weapons permit policy have all seen crime decrease after instituting the program.

Key Points

- School shootings have been prevented by guns and school officials with guns.
- Responsible gun owners and citizens have prevented many mass shootings from occurring.
- Many mass shootings occur in areas in which guns are not allowed, therefore, leaving a defenseless pool of people.
- States that have made it easier for possession of a concealed handgun permit have all witnessed violent crime decrease, as bad people are more hesitant to commit crimes.

Myth: Police Will Protect Us in Times of Massive Chaos and Riots

T o prove this myth wrong, I will allow history to speak for itself.

Many times in our country's history, there have been instances of riots and massive chaos whereby the police were ordered by state and federal troops to stand down and leave the area, for it was deemed "too dangerous."

Here are some of the major riots that have occurred in the past 50 years:

Newark Riots, 1967

Lasting almost a week, the Newark riots destroyed millions of dollars worth of businesses and real estate, and more than 26 people were killed.

Rodney King Riots, 1992

During these riots, 53 people were killed, more than 2,000 were injured, and more than one billion dollars in damages were incurred.

New York Draft Riots, 1863

A precursor to the Civil War, New York erupted into massive numbers of brawls, in which between 100 and 2,000 people were killed.

Chicago Riots at the Democratic National Convention, 1968

Tens of thousands of protestors spilled onto the Chicago streets and pillaged hundreds of businesses. Millions of dollars in property damages were recorded.

Detroit Riots, 1967

The Detroit riots are a fascinating example of how events can escalate out of control. I will go into great detail of these events so you can see how this could very well occur today.

Also known as the 12th Street Riots, the Detroit Riots were a public disorder that quickly turned into massive and violent public disturbances. They began on an early Saturday morning on July 23, 1967. Some Detroit policemen raided a local after-hours club, which incited much controversy among the neighborhood. Police were confronted by some of the patrons and observers, eventually evolving into one of the deadliest and most destructive riots in United States history.

As the riots grew on Sunday morning, police began getting pelted by rocks and stones thrown from rooftops. As the mob grew and became more disorderly, they started massive looting and general vandalism on 12th Street. It took the Detroit police almost five hours after the beginning of the riots to make the first arrest because of the number of looters and the lack of policemen. Because it was Sunday morning and the riots occurred very early in the morning, the state police were completely taken off guard and unable to assemble the ground force necessary to contain the mob.

The police tried several sweeps of 12th Street, all of which proved to be unsuccessful. When the rioters saw the ineffectiveness of the police, more bystanders joined in on the looting and the resistance against the police.

Around 2:30 p.m., the first major fire broke out at the cross streets of Atkinson and 12th. The growing mob prevented firefighters from putting out the fire.

Initially, the media and news stations did not report the violence or the looting. They were trying to prevent copycat mobs and riots. This too proved to be unsuccessful, for the looting and mobs moved way beyond the original location and the riots spread all over the city.

On Monday, July 24, the riots had escalated to another level, and the Detroit police called in the Michigan State Police force. As the looting and vandalism spread, the police were able to make more arrests as the day progressed. Because of the continuation of crime and lack of police, the people who were arrested were held in makeshift prisons, without proper documentation. Many people that were arrested that day either escaped and rejoined the mob or were never tried because of lack of evidence.

As the mob grew and collateral damage increased, an internal bureaucratic struggle broke out between then Michigan Governor George Romney and President Johnson. Johnson could not send in troops until the governor had declared Detroit in a "state of insurrection." This was because of the Insurrection Act of 1807, which stated that the federal government cannot deploy troops to ease civil unrest unless the local and state governments both surrender their jurisdiction of the locality in exchange for aid for the greater good.

Unfortunately, whenever crisis or disaster strikes, partisan politics usually takes the front seat, while public safety is not the first priority. Romney was suiting up for a presidential run on the Republican ticket, and Johnson did not want to commit troops only on Romney's direction, which would make a bad political image.

In addition to the governor/president partisan strife, the mayor of Detroit, Jerome Cavanagh, had his own political clash with Romney. Cavanagh was a Democrat who waited until the very last minute to reluctantly ask Romney for state aid.

All the way up the chain of command there was massive bureaucracy and partisan politics that got in the way of public safety. All throughout this time Detroit was being pillaged and plundered.

By Monday, 12th Street had more than 483 fires, and 231 more incidents were reported per hour. Arson and looting of businesses became more widespread as the day went on. Even black-owned community businesses were looted and burned to the ground. After the riot a black business owner said, "It does not matter what color you were; if you owned a place of business, they were coming for you."

During the course of the riots more than 2,498 rifles and 38 handguns were stolen from local stores. The Detroit and Michigan police forces were pushed out of the city for a second time, as they were unable to restore order. Shooting was common.

On late Monday night, President Johnson ordered federal troops to intervene and restore peace in Detroit. Nearly 3,700 federal paratroopers came into the city and helped clean up the streets through mostly violent means.

After the federal troops came into the city, it took almost 30 hours to completely end the riots. The violence escalated to its highest level and then slowly died down every hour. The mob had little organization, and by using military tactics the federal troops were able to disassemble the mob violence. Troops leveled many buildings that looters held.

Almost five days after the beginning of the riots, President Johnson officially called them to an end. For more than 100 hours Detroit had been under a state of chaos and anarchy. Police were unable to keep order, and other governmental action was ineffective as a result of partisan politics and a disorganized police force. Ten years later bullet holes on buildings were still common.

Imagine being a business owner in downtown Detroit and being unable to defend yourself or your family. Imagine being a single mother on the fifth floor of an apartment and seeing the mob climb the stairs toward your family. During periods of civil unrest, the only person that will defend you and your family is you.

As much as politicians try to paint a picture that the government and police will always be able to keep the peace, their entire argument is built on a house of cards. During the riots, the business owners who owned guns and had means of protecting themselves were able to deter rioters from pillaging their businesses.

There have been many times in our country's history that cities and towns have been overthrown. When the government is not able to step in effectively and protect your family or business, then who will protect you? The right and the ability to defend ourselves is fundamental to protecting our freedoms as we enjoy them, and this has been proven extensively when we look at the history of riots in this country and the other times when government loses its ability to protect the citizenry.

The people of Texas lost a battle to the Mexican General Santa Anna in 1847 and weeks later witnessed Santa Anna kill hundreds of men who had surrendered. Only armed Texans were able to defeat Santa Anna in Houston some months later. It is quite a tribute and fact that well armed ranches and civilians bested an army of a foreign country.

Key Points

- The Second Amendment states "the right to bear arms," not the privilege but the right.

- Texas lost the Alamo to Mexico in 1847, but Texas with arms defeated the Mexican general Santa Anna later in Houston and regained the land because they bore arms.

- There have been many times in our country's history for which the government has not been able to stop riots or protect its citizens.

- Business owners with guns are able to protect their businesses in times of rioting or looting.

- The Detroit Riots are a good example of why we need the Second Amendment to protect ourselves.

- The Second Amendment is the firewall for our basic freedoms and liberties.

Myth: Hunting Disrupts Animal Migration

Here's an argument from PETA's website: "Hunting also disrupts migration and hibernation patterns and destroys families. For animals such as wolves and geese, who mate for life and live in close-knit family units, hunting can devastate entire communities."

Unfortunately on its website, PETA does not go into detail or defend its claim that hunting "disrupts migration," nor does it defend its claim that hunting disrupts "hibernation patterns." By issuing this statement PETA demonizes the entire hunting community by eluding to the fact that not just hunting but hunters have also contributed to migratory patterns being skewed and hibernation cycles being disrupted.

To easily refute this myth, let's look at one of the most influential hunting and conservation groups in existence today: Ducks Unlimited. The purpose behind Ducks Unlimited quickly dismisses these false notions as put forth by PETA.

The Ducks Unlimited Success Story: How Hunters Saved Waterfowl

It was 1937, just seven years after the Great Depression, and the disastrous Dust Bowl had dried up thousands of feeding areas for ducks across the Midwest. Hunters hesitated to even hunt or shoot ducks during this period of time.

Many seasoned hunters feared that because of this natural disaster waterfowl as they knew it might be permanently ended.

One hunter recalled during that period of time that "it wasn't worth getting up early anymore to go hunt. Why should I go to my favorite spots just to see empty skies?" The time quickly became known as the "Duck Depression."

The solution was bold and unheard of for its time. A small group of seasoned hunters and shooters from across America got together and put forth a substantive plan to rejuvenate the waterfowl population in North America. Their plan would transcend the U.S.–Canadian border in an attempt to bring back the waterfowl population to its earlier prominence.

Many hunters would spend hundreds, if not thousands of dollars, to bring waterfowl to their particular blinds. Their plan was to multiply the population over an entire continent, a plan completely unheard of for that time.

Trying to understand why the population was on the decline, they started massive surveys across Canada and the United States. These surveys established a baseline for the current population and gave them additional information into how the waterfowl migrated.

After carefully analyzing their research, they determined they needed to invest time and money into what was known as the "Duck Factory," or the Canadian wetlands. This is where a majority of the waterfowl went to feed and live during the year before the migration season.

The first year, Ducks Unlimited planned to cultivate more than 100,000 acres for conservation. They targeted three specific wetlands that they would work on to bring back waterfowl breeding.

They worked with local farmers to create more efficient irrigation techniques that would not drain as much water away from the breeding grounds. As Ducks Unlimited began to gain notoriety, the press began to say, "This is not just an organization for sport. But this is a group of people committed to truly saving a specific species, and making sure they are going to be there for the next generation. Their commitment to saving the migratory patterns of waterfowl and fostering them for their kids and grandkids has been unparalleled to this time."

After one year of work and just eight months in the field, Ducks Unlimited cultivated more than 110,000 acres of feeding and breeding grounds for waterfowl. All of this commitment and time resulted in vast multiplication of ducks and geese in the years that followed.

Ducks Unlimited expanded into more projects across North America, focusing specifically on conservation. Through the 1950s and 1960s, a huge wave of grassroots support came in for Ducks Unlimited. Hunters all across North America pitched in money, volunteered, gave up land, and helped in any way possible to further the conservation projects Ducks Unlimited was involved in.

In the early 1980s it became evident a strategy was needed for waterfowl that were stopping on their migratory patterns throughout North America. Studies were done to analyze migratory patterns, and lakes and reservoirs were restored in regions where waterfowl usually stopped on their way south. Ducks Unlimited began opening offices in various parts of the country so they could offer unique regionalized conservation techniques for ducks and geese that were migrating south or returning north.

Over 75 years of work and commitment, Ducks Unlimited has influenced more than 95 million acres for the benefit of waterfowl in North America. Rough figures show that Ducks Unlimited played an instrumental role in preserving and fostering close to one billion waterfowl. For this, more than half a million members every year give money, time, and energy to make sure waterfowl will be there for the next generation.

Hunting was the reason these initiatives were started. True conservationists are indeed hunters. It began with a handful of dedicated outdoorsmen who loved to shoot and who refused to accept the fact that autumn skies would not be filled with ducks and geese. They refused to accept that waterfowl would no longer be able to be hunted and enjoyed on a widespread scale.

Hunting does not "throw off migratory patterns" as PETA claims. In fact hunting and hunters have saved migratory patterns and actually improved them. As a result of the investments they have made in wetlands and marshes, there are now more ducks and geese in North America than at any other time in history.

In the 1930s hunters in Michigan voluntarily agreed to an increase in the cost of hunting licenses so the state of Michigan could buy a huge piece of land in central Michigan specifically for the habitat of elk. The property became known as the Pigeon River State Forest. Today, 80 years later, sportsmen hunt elk every year under controlled management of the Michigan Fish and Game Department. It is 95 acres and holds the largest elk herd east of the Mississippi River. This is a true success story, possible only because of the conservation of hunters. The country abounds with examples like this that anti-hunters just do not know how to respond to.

The truth is no species has been eradicated because of hunting, but rather hunters have saved most of wildlife as we know it today. The fees from hunting licenses pay for fish and wildlife departments and personnel in almost every state. No anti-hunting group has ever paid for state wildlife departments or officers to my knowledge.

Hunters historically are the most creative and committed conservationists. They are the ones who want to save the wildlife and game for the next generation. Ducks Unlimited is just one story of how hunters have come together and saved a group of animals from becoming endangered.

This same effort is being followed for elk, deer, and other wildlife as conservation easements across the country are increasing lands set aside for wildlife and nondevelopment. Huge amounts of property are channeled each year into irrevocable land designations.

Antihunters generally collect money to fight hunting efforts, which seems to be a bigger priority to them than to promote conservation. Ask an anti hunter to name three conservation programs they have promoted in the last five years and you will see the point. Ask an anti hunter how much money they have contributed to any state fish and wildlife department.

Key Points

- Hunters have spent hundreds of millions of dollars improving migratory patterns for waterfowl.

- If it were not for Ducks Unlimited, ducks and geese might have become extremely close to being endangered.

- Ducks Unlimited was started by hunters to preserve the sport for the next generation.

- Hunters are historically the most likely to commit to conservation.

- Hunting license fees pay for state fish and game departments and conservation studies and efforts by these wildlife officers. Anti-hunters want to enjoy wildlife managed by state fish and wildlife departments but never seem to contribute anything close to the money hunters contribute for this management.

Myth: We Have to End the "Gun Show Loophole"

"Closing the gun show loophole would be a big step forward
because that's 40% of the sales in this country."
— Ed Schultz, MSNBC

"We have got to end the gun show loophole."
— Mayor Cory Booker, Newark, New Jersey

Most gun grabbers and groups that oppose the Second Amendment use this common "40%" figure when talking about gun shows. They argue that 40% of all gun transactions occur at gun shows.

First, we must pick apart this overused statistic to find out whether there is any legitimacy behind it.

This 40% number that President Obama, Mayor Bloomberg, Ed Schultz, and members of the media use came from a survey conducted in 1997. If we examine this survey closely we will see that the statistic is greatly flawed.

The 40% number was based on a phone survey that only 251 people who bought firearms participated in. That's right—there were only 251 people polled in this survey that was taken more than 15 years ago. Of the small pool of 251, about 35% said they didn't or "probably" didn't obtain their guns from a licensed dealer. Since the margin of error was +/–6 percentage points, it was rounded up to 40%, although using the same logic it could have easily been rounded down to 30 percent.

And of that near 40%, the poll showed that 29% of those gun owners got their guns from family members or friends. That leaves just 11% of firearms obtained in ways that would be frowned upon, if you accept the 40% number in the first place. Of the 11%, 3% said they got their guns through the mail, a process that requires full background checks. Therefore, you are looking at an extremely small number of people who were polled, and of that small pool of people, an extremely small percentage got their guns from a gun show. The final numbers concluded that about 4% of the people polled did obtain a firearm from a gun show.

Another survey done four years later, in 2001, by the Justice Department found that 0.7% of prison inmates on state and federal levels bought their weapons at a gun show.

People who criticize and attack gun shows have little or no understanding of how they work. All federal firearms licensees are required to conduct a background check for all firearm transactions, even if they sell a firearm at a gun show. This is under the National Instant Criminal Background Check Systems (NICS). This is to ensure that a gun is not being sold to a person who is prohibited under law from purchasing a gun. Such persons would include individuals who are severely mentally ill and people who have records of domestic violence. Yes, even at gun shows these background checks are required for guns sold by a federal firearm licensee. These checks are not required for an individual selling a used rifle or shotgun. Handguns have to be registered to the new owners even if they were purchased from individuals, being the new owners' responsibility.

People who fear gun shows just don't understand them. One of my friends asked me whether gun shows are where everyone brings their guns to a convention center and trades with each other. Not quite, I told him. Gun shows are actually very organized and have strict rules under which they must operate. The large majority of the vendors at the shows are fully licensed, and they are required to run approved FBI background checks at the time of sale.

Anti-gun advocates are really trying to stop private transactions that happen without government involvement, when in reality, a majority of those transactions happen between family members and neighbors. It is impossible to legislate or even design policy that would regulate every single time a grandparent gives a rifle to his or her grandson or granddaughter. Not only is it impossible, it would be an extremely foolish and intrusive policy. Yet gun grabbers advocate for every single gun to be registered and each transaction overseen, despite the avalanche of evidence that this is not where the problem lies.

Key Points

- The main argument against gun shows uses an outdated and inaccurate statistic.
- Less than 1% of criminals get their guns from gun shows.
- All gun show transactions by a licensed federal firearm licensee are subject to FBI background checks.
- Many people fear gun shows because of rumors and false notions they have been told.

Myth: Hunting Contributes to Violence in Our Society

"**I** believe that hunting desensitizes the hunter to pain, suffering and death, and that this lessening of what may be a natural compassion for other living creatures is not limited to non-human animals. I further believe that this inability to empathize is not healthy for members of a society trying to live together in peace and indeed, is not healthy for a society and its relations with other political entities in the world."—Dr. Priscilla Cohn, The Committee to Abolish Sport Hunting

Anti-hunters usually spread this myth with little to no factual evidence to back it up. It is more of an assumption than it is a fact. To disprove Dr. Cohn's bold claim, first, I will paint a picture of how hunters truly view hunting and killing, and then I will provide some actual scientific data that show her assumption to be false.

People who know hunters or who have spent time with hunters know that they are usually very responsible citizens. To hunt regularly it takes a rather substantial monetary investment, which most of the time means you are responsible in many facets of life. Dr. Cohn presents the argument that hunters lose compassion for animals after years of hunting. In fact, she says, this desensitization bleeds over into human relations.

Most hunters I know and have had the pleasure of meeting are some of the most mild-mannered and responsible people in the country. And almost all of them have a common thread that ties them together: a love for wildlife and their families. Almost all hunters own dogs and treat them like their own children. Contrary to what Dr. Cohn argues, hunters do not abuse animals they come into contact with; in fact, it's the opposite. They develop a deeper appreciation for wildlife through their hunting experiences. They learn more about the unique qualities of wildlife and consider hunting an animal to be a testament to its beauty and greatness.

For example, some of the top hunters in the world have trophies of big game they have shot in Africa. When you ask them about the animal, they don't say, "That stupid thing on the wall, I can't wait to shoot another one of those things." Instead, they say something along the lines of "The lion on the wall was the most dangerous and most difficult species I have ever harvested. It was the accumulation of all my hunting knowledge and preparation. The deer on the wall took me two years to learn its habitat and trails. It was a real challenge to get close enough to collect it with a bow."

Another misconception that anti-hunters commonly hold about hunting and violence is that they think hunters shoot everything they see. That is not even close to being true.

Award winner and one of the top hunters in the history of the sport, Tom Hammond said, "I can't even tell you how many hunts I have been on where I never pulled the trigger. Sometimes I just did not believe the trophy worthy. Other times the situation was not right. It is not about the killing. It is about being outside and enjoying nature. Most trophy hunters can remember the story behind each animal they harvest. It is the experience."

Another seasoned hunter of Africa, Mike Miller tells a story of one time when he went hunting in Africa:

> I arose early one day right at daybreak, and in the distance under a tree I saw a mother leopard playing with her newborn babies. I made my way over behind a bush where she could not see me. Seeing her play with her cubs under the tree it seemed as if they were almost smiling at each other. Every night I went over to that tree, and I left a little piece of meat for the baby leopards to climb up and eat. I woke up earlier each morning to go over there and see what the baby leopards would do that morning. I got so much joy from seeing the leopards grow up in front of my eyes as they showed great perseverance to continually go up the tree with all their willpower just to get the piece of meat I left for

them. I knew I was in great risk, for if the mother knew I was close, I may have been a dead man. It never even crossed my mind to shoot the mom. Some things are just too beautiful to kill.

Both of those stories are from some very experienced hunters. They have killed many kinds of game across the world, yet contrary to Dr. Cohn's claim, they don't develop a pleasure for killing or lose a sense of beauty and appreciation for those things around them.

To go into the other part of Dr. Cohn's statement and to dive deeper into this myth, I will talk more about whether hunting affects human relationships.

Luckily, there have been many studies that have directly dealt with the issue of violence and hunting. Perhaps the most relevant to this myth was a study done by Chris Eskridge, a criminologist from Nebraska.

Eskridge concluded at the end of his study that as hunting license sales go up, violent crime goes down. He even calculated population density and income levels into the study, to make the study more fair and balanced. He argued that hunting serves as a constructive outlet for many types of stress and tensions that otherwise could contribute to violent behavior.

More research came out after his study to back up his claim, which simply verified that when people enjoy more sport shooting, they also may enjoy more peace and increased social stability.

A world-renowned criminologist from Florida State, Gary Kleck stated after years of research that "gun owners are not, as a group, psychologically abnormal, nor are they more racist, sexist, or pro-violent than non-owners are."

According to a study of high school students in Rochester, New York, by Lizotte and Sheppard, students who were taught to use a gun and owned a gun legally and had parental supervision had lower rates of crime, drug use, and delinquency than did their peers who had never come across guns before in their lives.

Many studies have shown that almost 70% of hunters are motivated to hunt each year because they have a psychological connection with nature that they feel is exclusive to hunting. Some even said they believe hunting helps improve their mental health.

The science and real-life examples are not on the side of the anti-hunters. It is simple—hunting is a natural part of life. Studies have shown that there are more positives that come out of hunting than negatives in terms of mental health. Even looking at crime trends, Eskridge's study shows that when hunting licenses go up, crime goes down.

It is important to remember that people who say that hunting contributes to violence in society usually don't have a great understanding of hunting or hunters.

Key Points

- A recent five-year study showed the sales nationwide of hunting licenses increasing.
- Not every hunt results in a kill.
- Hunters have a deep appreciation for wildlife.
- Studies show that areas in which there are more hunting licenses have less crime.
- Students who were taught about guns from an early age are less likely to engage in drugs and alcohol.
- Hunting has many positive psychological benefits, including stress release.
- Hunters do not become desensitized to life just because of hunting; in fact, they learn to appreciate it more.

Myth: Magazine Limits Would Prevent Mass Shootings and Bring Down Crime

"The time has come, America, to step up and ban these weapons. The other very important part of this bill is to ban large capacity ammunition feeding devices, those that hold more than 10 rounds. We have federal regulations and state laws that prohibit hunting ducks with more than three rounds. And yet it's legal to hunt humans with 15-round, 30-round, even 150-round magazines. Limiting magazine capacity is critical because it is when a criminal, a drug dealer, a deranged individual has to pause to change magazines and reload that the police or brave bystanders have the opportunity to take that individual down."

—Senator Diane Feinstein, California

For decades Senator Feinstein has led the charge for magazine limits and the "assault weapon ban." She uses the same talking points over and over again to push her anti-gun and big-government agenda. This quote she gave before Congress in January 2013 is filled with falsehoods and misleading statements, so we will start there.

It is pretty obvious human hunting is not legal, so there is no need to dissect that part of the myth, but interestingly enough she brings in duck hunting ammunition limits as a way to justify magazine restrictions. Let's first analyze what the law is regarding duck hunting, then let's look at why the law is that way, then we can come to a conclusion as to whether Senator Feinstein's argument has any validity.

As stated previously in this book, the 1930s were a very scary time for waterfowl and duck hunting. The game was being depleted not because of hunting but because of the Dust Bowl and other environmental factors taking place in western and southern Canada. Because of the low numbers of ducks in the skies, federal and state officials began instituting ammo restrictions on magazine limits on shotguns to prevent what was called "cloud busting." Essentially if a flock of ducks or geese began migrating south, some hunters would spray countless rounds into the sky to down as many birds as possible. Since the duck population was on a steep decline, measures were taken to prevent this sort of abuse from occurring. After its implementation in the 1930s hunters have kept the restrictions in place as a way to validate the sport. As some of the best hunters have put it, "Where's the fun if you can spray 30 rounds at a duck? Three rounds make it competitive and fun." And that is the way duck and goose hunting is still done today.

So now that we know the history of duck ammo restrictions, let's go back to Senator Feinstein's reasoning for ammo restrictions.

Under her logic, she believes that most mass shootings and gun crime could be prevented with the implementation of her magazine limit. Contrary to what she wants you to believe, mass shootings are not always done with high-capacity magazines or guns. Let's take the Virginia Tech and Columbine shootings. All three shooters in both of the massacres used 10-round magazines, but they just brought lots of them to reload. Under Senator Feinstein's gun ban, 10-round magazines would be legal, thus her "solution" would not have prevented those massacres from occurring. Even with the Aurora, Colorado, movie theater massacre, the shooter's gun, which had a 100-magazine limit, jammed. This occurrence is common with high-level magazine guns that shoot at rapid-fire rates, as they have a higher likelihood to jam or overheat.

Also when talking about magazine restrictions or gun bans, it's important to get all the facts regarding the people making the argument. Senator Feinstein's solution is to put a ban on magazines that hold anything over 10 rounds. That may sound like it would make some logical sense, but people who understand and use guns know that the 10-round limit is a completely arbitrary number.

AR-15 type rifles come from the manufacturers with devices that feed between 15 and 30 rounds, and some even hold more. It all depends on their design and purpose. Ten is a number that is pulled literally out of thin air. Gun grabbers have no logical purpose to support a 10-magazine limit, except for political advancement of a greater anti-gun agenda. Most anti-gun proponents will say that higher-capacity magazines allow murderers to kill more people, but that is not the case.

The Department of Justice conducted a study in 2004 that stated that "assailants fire less than four shots on average, a number well within the 10-round magazine limit." The DOJ study confirms that Senator Feinstein's gun ban is not based on logic or factual data but instead on an ulterior political agenda.

In an interview with the *Washington Times*, Lawrence Keane, senior vice president and general counsel of the National Shooting Sports Foundation said, "Studies prove that the arbitrary magazine capacity restriction that was in place for a decade did not reduce crime." He continued, "In searching for effective means to reduce violence, we should not repeat failed policies, especially when they infringe on the constitutional rights of the law-abiding."

Keane is talking specifically about the assault weapons ban that expired in 2004. This ban was imposed by the federal government for a 10-year period. Since the ban expired, violent crime has decreased by more than 17%, a significant improvement. Completely arbitrary ammo restrictions and gun bans do nothing but put a strain on good, law-abiding citizens who want to defend themselves. Earlier in this book I detailed the value that AR-15s offer young women who want to defend themselves. Under Senator Feinstein's gun ban, AR-15s would be illegal.

Instead of trying to restrict ammo and ban guns on "fringe logic" and political motivations, gun grabbers should look at the massive amount of empirical evidence that shows assault weapon bans and ammo restrictions do not work and that all they do is disallow everyday people from protecting themselves and their families.

People unfamiliar with AR-15 type rifles should know they are not "automatic." Automatic means that if you hold the trigger back, the entire clip fires. Combat allows this. However, automatic rifles and adjustments to rifles to make them automatic are federal offenses. AR-15 type rifles used by citizens have to utilize a standard trigger—one pull for each shot fired. So you really cannot compare the AR-15 type rifle to those used by the military in warfare.

Key Points

- Comparing duck hunting restrictions to self-defense is not logically sound.
- Both the Virginia Tech and Columbine shootings were performed with weapons that would still be legal under Senator Feinstein's idea of magazine limitations.
- The average assailant uses less than four rounds in a murder.
- The 10-round magazine limit is completely arbitrary and does not apply to most firearms or feeders.

Myth: Hunting is Unusually Cruel and Most Animals Suffer Prolonged and Painful Deaths

"Quick kills are rare, and many animals suffer prolonged, painful deaths when hunters severely injure but fail to kill them."

—PETA's website

W henever addressing animal killing or hunting, it is first important to qualify your argument in the most compassionate and understanding manner possible. This is usually a very hot-button and sensitive issue among anti-hunters.

Most wild animals in nature don't pass away in comfort. They do not die a quick and sedated death with the help of veterinary medication. Instead, in nature, they usually die an extremely violent, agonizing death. Only through hunting is a quick and painless death possible to prevent the animals from being eaten to death. Animal and wildlife experts will tell you, nothing is more painful for an animal than for it to be eaten alive. An old pheasant does not normally die in its sleep. Instead it usually is caught by a hawk or fox and eaten, which is a long, painful death.

Professional hunters who have hunted in Africa have said that the most painful thing they have witnessed was to see a zebra be eaten alive by a pack of lions. It is a long process, as the lions literally chomp away, piece by piece, at the zebra. The alternative would be a quick bullet through the heart, ending the animal's life with dignity and honor.

PETA continues the argument on its website, attacking bow hunting as one of the biggest culprits for animal suffering. Many other anti-hunting groups are on campaigns to end bow hunting, for they find it to be "inhumane" and that it causes animals "undue suffering." An extremely intensive survey done out of Maryland by the Natural Resources Office in 2008 followed hunters and logged all of their bow hunting data for one year. Despite what many anti-hunting groups would tell you, an overwhelming majority of all bow hunters kill their targets without the animal getting away. The study found that bow hunters have an 89% accuracy rate of hitting their targets. They also found that 82% of all deer that were hit were found within a short distance. As the study went deeper into specific hunters, they found that hunters who hunt a lot have a recovery rate of almost 87%. Considering these hunters are aiming at live targets in real-life conditions, more than an 80% recovery rate seems to invalidate painful death claims.

Natural predatory death for animals is much more painful than death by a bow or bullet. Hunters do intensive research into exactly how to kill an animal to ensure the least amount of pain possible. Hunters do not find pleasure in seeing animals suffer, unlike what most anti-hunting advocates would tell you. People who hunt do everything humanly possible to make kills quick and safe and as respectful of nature and the wildlife as possible.

As a matter of fact, each year better bullets and arrowheads are manufactured. Today's advanced technology ensures today's hunters more accuracy, especially at distance, than hunters 20 years ago.

Key Points

- Predatory death for animals is one of the most painful ways for an animal to die.

- Hunters do kill a number of animals, but the death is usually swift and a lot faster than a predatory death they would probably experience if not killed by hunting.

- Hunters do everything they can to limit an animal's suffering.

- Quick kills are common among experienced hunters.

Link

http://www.marylandgdma.com/files/Download/Pedersen-31-34.pdf

Myth: Hunting Is Dangerous

Most of my friends who have never hunted before have this preconceived notion that hunting is extremely dangerous. I think it goes back to the old movie the *Christmas Story*, in which little Ralphie's mom continues to say throughout the movie, "You can't get a gun! You'll shoot your eye out!" Unfortunately, that narrative is perpetuated throughout childhood for many people, and they grow up believing that hunting is a very dangerous sport, filled with accidents and deaths.

On the outside, it would seem that hunting would be more prone to accidents than most other activities because most recreations don't use live firearms or ammunition. But the opposite is true. According to a recent study conducted by the National Safety Council, more people per 100,000 participants are injured while playing baseball or bicycling than while hunting. And an even more recent study shows that while about 100 people die nationwide in hunting-related accidents each year, more than 1,500 people die in swimming-related incidents.

The reason hunting is statistically safer than most other outdoor activities is the care and seriousness hunters put into gun safety and training. Most states require young hunters to pass a firearms safety course. In Minnesota, 4,000 volunteer instructors give firearms safety training to more than 20,000 young hunters each year.

Before the first time I was even allowed to go hunting or shooting, I was taught extremely important gun safety and then tested on it several times. Hunters do not take this lightly, and the best hunters will tell you that a safe hunt is the best hunt. When dealing with live firearms, joking around is not allowed nor should it be tolerated.

There are entire organizations dedicated to teaching firearm and hunting safety. One of these is the Weatherby Foundation, which hosts training sessions for families who want to teach their children about hunting and the importance of firearm safety.

A friend of mine and seasoned hunter from Montana, Mark Johnson has a unique family policy. He will take any of his seven kids bear hunting with him after they are 10 years old. But when they are in the field they are not allowed to have a loaded gun until their third year hunting. His kids are taught every necessity of safety when dealing with hunting. He has them walk through the hunts with him, seeing through example and practice exactly how to safely hunt and how to use a firearm.

I have yet to run across a hunter who does not value safety as the most important part of the sport. Statistics show that hunting is indeed safe, but whenever you hunt never compromise a shot for safety.

Be careful when hearing about deaths from hunting. Many are not a result of gun accidents. Many are heart related or other internal causes of death occurring while in the field.

Some countries even go to the extreme. In Germany, for example, it takes weeks of testing to get a hunting license. Hunting is a tradition in Europe, and many hunting regulations are patterned after European regulations in this country. Hunting is allowed in all or most European countries, including Russia.

One key point that anti hunters and our government never bring up is how well trained with weapons our young people going into the military are who had a history of hunting. It certainly is easier to train a man or woman who has been familiar with hunting weapons. Ask any military instructor when was the last time a non hunter was the most proficient in the classes designed around weaponry.

Key Points

- Hunting is painted as a dangerous sport and pastime, when in reality the exact opposite is true.
- Millions of dollars are spent every year to teach young people about firearm safety.
- Safety is the most important thing valued by hunters.

Myth: Hunting Is Only for Men

I find the narrative that women don't hunt entrenched into our society mostly because of popular culture. The media make it seem as though all hunters are old, white males. Granted, most hunters are males, but if you look at trends and statistics recently, they show that more women are beginning to take up the sport of hunting and competitive sports shooting. It's an exciting time to be a hunter, and many women are beginning to discover the beauty and complexity that come with hunting.

Unfortunately, women get perceived as people who would not be interested in hunting or shooting. Many young women sometimes never even get the chance to fire a rifle when growing up, for it may be looked down upon in their local community or culture. And even if many of these young women do take up hunting in their formative years, their friends are likely to tease or not accept them if they are avid hunters.

Despite these preconceived notions, in 2009 alone, more women took up hunting than did men according to the National Sporting Goods Association. In a single year, the number of female hunters increased by over 5.4%.

The increase in women hunters and shooters is obvious when you go to buy a gun today. You can easily find handguns that are specifically made for women that do not "kick" because of a big caliber.

"Women are buying more handguns, rifles, shotguns. We are the market of the future," said Judy Rhodes, the cofounder of DIVA-WOW (Women Outdoors Worldwide).

In Idaho alone, in 2010, females made up almost 20% of all hunting applications and license registrations. The same trends are being seen across the country, which show that more and more women are becoming avid hunters.

Over the past 10 years, if we analyze the growth in hunting among women, we see that the number of female hunters has risen by more than 42% from 2001 to 2011. In 2001 there were about 1.8 million female hunters, and now there are well over 2.6 million—an absolutely amazing increase over a short period of time.

As more women get into hunting, it is interesting to get feedback on their performance as hunters and shooters. Jim Toynbee, who has been teaching young hunters marksmanship for more than 40 years, is 100% convinced that girls are better shots than boys are.

"In almost every class I teach, girls will outshoot the boys," he said. Professional hunters and shooters who are female argue that women are able to outperform men because there are almost no societal expectations of them. No instructor or parent is going to expect a young girl to be a perfect shot, whereas men usually compare marksmanship directly to masculinity, therefore they feel more pressure when they shoot.

The best live pigeon shooter in the world, Stacie Segebart, has been beating the boys since the first time she picked up a rifle. Since a young age Stacie has been winning state and national championships in coed divisions. She has been embarrassing boy and men hunters her entire life—and she loves it.

To really prove the point about how many women hunt, just check the size of the women's department in outdoor sporting stores and outdoor apparel stores.

In the growing hunting sector among women, we are seeing some extremely vibrant and promising entrepreneurs arise from this drastic increase in women who are hunting. Kristin Pike started Preis Hunting and Field Apparel for Women in Gunnison, Colorado, in 2008.

"Basically, I became frustrated that there were no women's hunting clothes that were performance driven and athletic," said Pike. "We decided to go after that market and have had great success doing so."

Pike said sales more than doubled in 2010, and this year to date, Preis has seen a 400% sales growth. Preis sells its merchandise online and at retail shops.

A great example of a young woman defending the Second Amendment and organizing people for action is Regis Giles, from Miami, Florida. An extremely accomplished and avid hunter from a young age, Regis decided to start an organization that would give young women a voice in the media and in our schools to own guns. "Realizing my voice wasn't being heard by the media on the TV screen I had to do something. I had enough. I was tired of girls staying the victim. Knowing how to defined my life, I wanted to set a fire under the bottoms of ladies across the nation and help motivate them to do something."

She then decided to start a website and organization called Girls Just Wanna Have Guns. After building a small audience on Facebook and Twitter, it now has a national audience. Its website features young women from across the country who support gun ownership and the Second Amendment. She has successfully assembled women and begun to sway the narrative away from women being victims toward women being able to effectively defend themselves.

As hunters and lovers of the outdoors, these upward trends and positive increases among female hunters should give all people who enjoy the sport of hunting great promise and hope that the heritage of hunting will not die. Women are a growing part of the general U.S. population and are a quickly growing segment of the hunting population. In the fight to preserve hunting for the next generation, women will play an integral role in defending the sport we all love.

Key Points

- Female hunters have increased by more than 42% over the past 10 years.
- Women hunters are the fastest growing sector of hunting in the United States.
- More and more outfitters are catering to women hunters.
- According to some marksmen experts, women are better shots than men are.
- Female hunters will be instrumental for the success of hunting.

Links

http://www.ncwildlife.org/News/Blogs/NCWRCBlog/tabid/715/EntryId/30/Number-of-Women-Hunters-Steadily-Increases-in-North-Carolina.aspx

http://abcnews.go.com/Business/sarah-palin-effect-women-men-picking-hunting/story?id=13047758&page=2#.UeOZjlFzMTO

http://lancasteronline.com/sports/a-female-hunter-s-appeal/article_668bc9f4-b39d-5599-8d05-1f7bcdb8ce66.html

Myth: The Second Amendment Is Outdated and Unnecessary

"When they passed the Second Amendment, they had muskets. It took 20 minutes to load one, and half the time, you missed, OK? The Second Amendment didn't take into account assault weapons."

—Deepak Chopra, December 21, 2012

"In writing the Second Amendment, the Framers didn't envision the kind of gun toting that is permitted across this country today."

—Melynda Price, from the article "Get Rid of the Right to Bear Arms"

"I don't think the Founding Fathers had the idea that every man, woman, and child could carry an assault weapon."

—Mayor Michael Bloomberg, December 16, 2012

"There are complaints that the Second Amendment to the Constitution gives us a right to bear arms. That amendment was passed more than 200 years ago. We are now more than 200 years past that time in history. It was passed at a time when people were moving to frontiers in which a gun was necessary to defend one's property."

—Ruth Bowser, February 17, 2013

It seems whenever the Second Amendment comes under fire from gun grabbers, one of the most common arguments I hear is something along the lines of "The founding fathers wrote the Second Amendment in a different time, with different weapons."

To deconstruct this argument let's see whether this logic is relatable to the other amendments.

Let's take the First Amendment for example. Would anyone ever suggest that the First Amendment applies only to quill and paper? Or public speeches? I don't think there is any controversy that people have freedom of speech through using blogs, tweeting, emails, and television. So it is fair to say that the First Amendment has grown with and through the times, naturally adjusting with technology.

So the basis of their argument is, "When the founding fathers wrote the Constitution and the Second Amendment, times were so different; therefore the amendment included in the document cannot be relatable in today's society." Although we just proved that entire argument is wrong when applying that logic to the First Amendment. Technology advances and changes, and the purpose of the amendments stays the same. The First Amendment protects our right to freedom of speech and press. The founding fathers added this because under the rule of the British Empire, freedoms of speech and press were being suppressed. No one with any legitimacy is arguing that we should suppress the First Amendment or get rid of it. Then why doesn't this same thought process and perspective apply to the Second Amendment?

If we read the Second Amendment closely, it is hard to miss the genius and foresight the founders possessed when writing our founding documents. Instead of writing "the right of the people to bear muskets, swords, and flintlock pistols," they simply wrote "the right to bear arms." When reflecting on what they wrote, it is evident that the founders understood technology and innovation occur at such a fast rate that to make this document truly capture human activity they included a broader term, such as "bear arms." One of my favorite quotes regarding the Constitution is, "The founders did not write the constitution for the times. They wrote it to stand the test of time."

To reinforce this point that the Second Amendment is not just for the times but rather timeless, let's look at what the Supreme Court had to say. In the landmark 2008 ruling, the Supreme Court came to the very same conclusion in the case of *District of Columbia v Heller*. The court observed:

> Some have made the argument, bordering on the frivolous, that only those arms in existence in the 18th century are protected by the Second Amendment. We do not interpret constitutional rights that way. Just as

the First Amendment protects modes of communications e.g. Reno v ACLU, 521 U.S. 844, 849 (1997), and the fourth amendment applies to modes forms of search e.g. Kyllo v United States, 533 U.S. 27, 35-36 (2001), the second amendment extends, prima facie, to all instruments that constitute bearable arms, even those that were not in existence at the time of the founding.

The court made it clear that this anticonstitutional argument perpetuated by gun grabbers is borderline "frivolous." Yes, it is frivolous, for it is truly an argument that is not logically sound in any regard.

In addition to the court's ruling, I think that to properly defend the Second Amendment and its purpose in the 21st century, we have to fully understand why the founding fathers decided to put it in our constitution. Despite what many textbooks and teachers may tell you, the Second Amendment is not for hunting nor is it purely for self-defense either.

There are many reasons the Second Amendment was written and put into the Constitution. Many of those reasons are detailed in this book. But I want to reinforce the underlying reason the Second Amendment exists and needs to continue to exist as long as we consider ourselves free people. The basis and philosophical reasoning for having a Second Amendment is to allow the citizens to protect themselves against a tyrannical government. The right to bear arms allows the people to be able to resist government tyranny. As I will detail more in the upcoming chapters, democracy is riddled with examples of governments going tyrannical. The only firewall between a tyrannical government and the freedom and liberties of its people is the ability of the people to fight back against that government's aggression. And that underlying belief has never been and will never be outdated.

Key Points

- The Constitution was not written for the times. It was written to stand the test of time.
- Saying the Second Amendment pertains only to muskets is like saying the First Amendment applies only to quill and paper.

- The purpose of the Second Amendment is to allow the citizens to resist tyranny and forms of tyrannical government.
- In the famous court case *District of Columbia v Heller*, the Supreme Court ruled that constitutional rights are not subject to the time in which they were written.
- The Second Amendment provides the people an unrestricted, unaltered, and undeniable "RIGHT" to bear arms.

Myth: The United Kingdom and Australia Are Seeing Lower Crime Rates Because of Increased Gun Control

"Gun control has worked very successfully in Great Britain, in Australia, and in Japan."

—Piers Morgan, December 17, 2012

"Australia is an excellent example [of gun control]. In 1996, a 'pathetic social misfit,' as a judge described him, was the lone who killed 35 people with a spray of bullets from semi-automatic weapons. Within weeks, the Australian government was working on gun reform laws that banned assault weapons and shotguns, tightened licensing and financed gun amnesty and buyback programs."

—*New York Times* editorial, December 17, 2012

"If there is one country that best represents the possibility of cutting gun crime by increasing gun control, it is Australia."

—Nick Schifrin, ABC News, December 19, 2012

W hen listening to the news and hearing people like Piers Morgan and Nick Schifrin commend Australia and Britain for their policy subscriptions to gun crime, it almost sounds convincing. Leave it to the media to try to sway the population into buying into this false narrative about guns and violent crime.

First, let's start with the facts.

Yes, Britain and Australia have lower incidents of gun homicides and crime than those in the United States. That's because over the past 40 years Britain has slowly eroded away the right and ability for private citizens to own guns. Finally, in 1997, The Firearms Act banned guns almost entirely in the United Kingdom. Owning a gun today in the United Kingdom is nearly impossible and requires you to prove to the local police a "necessity." Sport hunters can have guns.

In Australia it's very simple. They don't have nor ever have had a bill of rights similar to ours. Therefore, gun ownership has not been part of the natural fabric of Australian culture. So, in 1996, Australia moved toward a unilateral blanket gun ban. Both countries now have some of the strictest gun laws in the world. And, on the cursory, it seems that gun control has worked for both the United Kingdom and Australia. But the mistake Piers Morgan, the *New York Times*, and Nick Schifrin are all making is that they are not looking at overall crime. They have tunnel vision and are focused just on gun crime, which is preventing them from seeing how massive gun confiscation has resulted in huge spikes in overall crime.

As to not confuse each country's statistics, we will examine each country one at a time. First, we begin with the United Kingdom.

United Kingdom

Despite the rosy picture painted by the mass media and politicians, the United Kingdom is far from the safe haven they make it out to be. Yes, as stated above, their gun crime is significantly lower than that in the United States. That is because literally no guns are owned by citizens and there are restrictions on ammunition that would make your head spin. But what about overall crime? Did total gun confiscation work to lower the entire crime footprint?

The easy answer to that is a resounding NO. This past year, new and alarming data show that more than 1,000 people a month in London alone are victims of knife crimes. These new statistics were obtained after a freedom of information request, which revealed that there were 1,038 victims of knife crimes in January 2013—just *one* month in *one* city.

Many residents of London are extremely fearful at night and are beginning to see the emergence of street gangs in seemingly nice areas. The founder of the youth charity Kids Company said that knife crime levels in London are still extremely high. "We do not see any signs that violence among young people on the street is going down."

A brutal example showing the extent of knife crimes is a shopkeeper named Ashok Patel, who was stabbed repeatedly in the head as he bravely defended his shop from armed knife thieves last December.

Mr. Patel grabbed a baseball bat to fend off the burglars. He then proceeded to fall, and the raiders pounced on him, using kitchen knives to stab his head, stomach, and hand, and then left him for dead.

Luckily, he survived as a result of the marvels of modern medicine. He said in a statement later, "I wanted to save my life and my shop, so I shouted at them and took up my baseball bat. I was very scared, and they stabbed me in my head and stomach. My head still goes round and round, and I can't move my left arm very well."

The streets of London have almost never been more dangerous. Tourists are popular targets for the knife gangs, for they are more likely to carry money and are usually unarmed. Typically, the knife gangs will come up behind you and slice you at the sides of your stomach, leaving you gasping for air as they grab your wallet and belongings. Not a pretty sight to witness.

A direct comparison of the United Kingdom and United States regarding violent crime shows that the United Kingdom had 933 violent crimes per 100,000 people in 2012. Comparatively, the United States had a violent crime rate of 399 per 100,000 people. That is a stark difference for a country that is supposedly leading the charge in terms of crime rates. These figures were published by the Institute for Economics and Peace.

Australia

As stated above, Australia instituted extremely cumbersome and strict gun laws after a massacre that occurred in Tasmania in 1996. The government of Australia sponsored a huge buyback program for almost all guns within a couple of months. Before the buyback and gun confiscation program, gun homicides were averaging about 82 a year. After the buyback program they dropped to 58 per year. Did they go down a bit? Yes, but it was not a drastic decrease. The government confiscated and bought back more than 650,000 guns in two years. So, for every 30,000 guns confiscated, one gun homicide was prevented. To be speculative, let's say each person owned two guns. Therefore 15,000 people were less safe and disarmed for every gun homicide that was prevented. Seems like this massive government overhaul of guns did not exactly have the potent impact the government expected it would have.

Just like in the United Kingdom, it is important to realize there is a categorical difference between gun crime and overall crime. Too often the media, either intentionally or unintentionally, misreports and confuses the two. Before the gun ban in Australia non-gun homicides averaged about 240 per year from 1991 to 1996. After the ban, homicides increased to 255 per year from 1997 to 2001.

A study conducted by Wang-Shen Lee and Sandy Suardi, of the Melbourne Institute of Applied Economic and Social Research at the University of Melbourne, concluded that the "results of these tests suggest that the NFA [the 1996–1997 National Firearms Agreement] did not have any large effects on reducing firearms homicide or suicide rates."

A deeper analysis into Australian crime after the gun ban shows us that armed robberies went from about 6,000 in 1996 to around 10,000 between 1998 and 2001. Essentially, fewer guns in the hands of private citizens results in a drastic increase in crime.

The Bottom Line

The United States has a culture significantly different from that of Britain or Australia. We have a radically different perspective on gun ownership and also a different view on individual liberty and freedom. Whenever someone claims that the United Kingdom and Australia have been shining examples for how gun control will curb crime, you have an obligation to correct that individual and illustrate the fundamental difference between gun crime and overall crime.

As mentioned earlier, numerous states have made it easier to have a concealed weapon permit. In each of these states violent crime has decreased. Most states have witnessed an increased sale of firearms to women, including handguns.

Key Points

- It is important to know the difference between gun crime and overall crime.
- London is regarded as the "knife crime of Europe."
- The United Kingdom had 933 violent crimes per 100,000 people in 2012. Comparatively, the United States had a violent crime rate of 399 per 100,000 people.
- In Australia, for every 30,000 guns confiscated, one gun homicide was prevented.
- The United States has massive cultural differences from the United Kingdom and Australia. In addition, our country was founded with rights to the people and the right to bear arms was one of them. The Second Amendment is a cornerstone to our constitution and requirement of government to uphold.

Myth: Gun Control in the United States Results in Lower Gun Crime

"The answer is not more guns. A trendy argument suggests we'll be safer
if more people carry guns. It's dangerous, wrong and terrible policy."
—Alex Seitz-Wald, Salon.com, December 17, 2012

"So, as the times change so do our laws and today we can rely on the
fact that less guns equals less crime."
—Forrest Freeman, Yahoo! contributor network, January 12, 2007

Only a few pieces of evidence are needed to dispel this myth, and all it takes is to look no further than Chicago. In 2012 alone, Chicago had more than 500 gun-related deaths. To put it in different terms, more people died in Chicago than the troops we lost fighting in Afghanistan in 2012.

These numbers are completely unacceptable and saddening for the people of Chicago. But who is to blame for the rapid escalation of all this violence? It is very simple: gun control. Up until July 2013, it was illegal to carry a concealed handgun in the state of Illinois.

Illinois is the only state in the union that has not allowed concealed carry. In addition, the city of Chicago forbids and has banned the possession and ownership of assault weapons.

And that is not all for Chicago. Gun shops are also outlawed in the city of Chicago. Handguns were banned in Chicago for decades until 2010, when the U.S. Supreme Court overturned that ruling. Chicago also disallows civilian gun ranges and bans high-capacity magazines.

Even with all of these gun laws that have been instituted throughout the years, gun crime and overall crime in Chicago is consistently on the upswing. Certain blocks of Chicago are more dangerous than war-torn Kabul, Afghanistan.

Yet, the good law-abiding citizens of Chicago are not legally allowed to defend themselves against the murder spree that is plaguing America's second city. The only thing increased gun control has done for the city of Chicago is give gangs and criminals a leg up, for they now know that the majority of the population in Chicago is unarmed.

Before Chicago's ban in 1982, the murder rate per 100,000 people was falling from 27 to 22 in the prior five years; suddenly it stopped falling and rose to 23 in the five years following. John Lott sums it up succinctly: "Chicago's murder rate fell from being 8.1 times greater than its neighbors in 1977 to 5.5 times in 1982, and then went way up to 12 times raster in 1987."

Let's look at Houston, Texas, a city that is similar in its makeup to Chicago in terms of demography and density and see what affect gun crime has had on it. Like Chicago, Houston is a major center for illegal activities, such as the drug trade and massive human trafficking. Despite both cities being entrenched in crime, Houston has a murder rate that is two thirds that of Chicago. Why is this? It's because the people of Houston are allowed to be well armed, while innocent people in Chicago are defenseless against the constant siege of attacks.

Another example of how U.S. gun control laws have failed miserably in lowering crime is Washington, D.C. In 1977 the DC handgun ban went into effect. Since its implementation, there has been only one year (1985) during which the city's murder rate fell below what it was during the years leading up to the ban. Even after the ban, DC's murder rate ranked in the top four among the 50 largest U.S. cities in 19 of those years. Before the ban was implemented, DC was never ranked even close to that high. It only ranked in the top 15 once.

It's important when examining strict gun control laws to not just look at cities but entire states. In the two previous examples, Chicago and DC, both cities have attributes and population numbers that mirror those of many states. Massachusetts instituted strict gun control measures and, after doing so, experienced escalations in gun crime, as well as overall crime.

In 1998 Massachusetts passed a law that made it very difficult to own a gun and banned semiautomatic "assault weapons" outright. The laws did work in making it very hard for law-abiding citizens to own a gun, but it had no affect on people who generally ignore laws. Another term for those people is "criminals." In 1998 before the intrusive gun policy there were 1.5 million active licenses to own guns and just 200,000 four years later.

In 2011 Massachusetts had more than 120 firearm homicides. This was according to the *Boston Globe*, which called it "a striking increase from the 65 in 1998." Almost all other categories of violent crime went up as well. Aggravated assault went up 26.7%, and armed robbery was up 20.7%.

If we look at Massachusetts in a regional comparison, we find that before the ban was instituted in Massachusetts the lowest ever per capita murder rate was in 1997, but by 2011 it had increased 47%, beating the national trend, which was going down. During that same time period, the national trend went down 31%, while Massachusetts' rate went up 47%.

Now that we know Massachusetts had failed policies in comparison to previous years, let's compare it to neighboring states. In 1998 we find that Massachusetts had a gun murder rate that was roughly 70% higher than that of other neighboring states (Vermont, New Hampshire, Rhode Island, Connecticut, New York, Maine). Recent data show that homicides in Massachusetts are 125% higher than the average of the other neighboring states.

As you can see from these statistics, these are three prime examples of how states and cities try to curb gun violence by banning many types of guns and making it nearly impossible to own one. They have failed miserably in protecting innocent people who want to defend themselves. It is very simple: the more we restrict our right to bear arms, the more opportunity we give criminals to commit crime.

As stated earlier in this book, all states that have made it easier to have a concealed weapon permit have witnessed a decrease in crime.

Key Points

- Chicago has the strictest gun control in the country, yet one of the highest murder rates.

- More people died in Chicago from gun crime than U.S. troops died in Afghanistan in 2012.

- Gun ranges and high-capacity magazines are illegal in Chicago, as well as concealed weapon permits.

- Houston, a city similar to Chicago in population and drug crime, has a murder rate that is two thirds that of Chicago's.

- After the DC gun ban went into effect in 1977, it has had only one year that had less gun crime than the years before the ban.

- After Massachusetts instituted the assault weapons gun ban, crime went up 125% in comparison to neighboring states.

- By 2011 gun crime in Massachusetts was up 47% while the national trend was going dramatically down.

Myth: U.S. Gun Crime Is Increasing

T his may be the easiest myth in the entire book to refute. Despite public opinion and fear mongering by the media, statistics do not lie.

According to a study released by the FBI, gun-related homicides and crime are "strikingly" down from 20 years ago. A new study by the Pew Research Center shows that U.S. gun homicides rose in the 1960s, gained in the 1970s, peaked in the 1980s and the early 1990s, and then plunged and leveled out over the past 20 years.

The researchers say, "Despite national attention to the issue of firearm violence most Americans are unaware that gun crime is lower today than it was two decades ago."

Another Pew Survey in March found that 56% believed that gun-related crime is higher now than it was 20 years ago. Only 12% of the people polled said that it is lower, 26% believed it was about the same, and 6% said they do not know.

The study found that firearm-related homicides climaxed in 1993 at 7.0 deaths per 100,000 people. But the study found that by 2010 the rate was an amazing 49% lower and that firearm-related violence was 75% lower in 2011 than in 1993. These are statistics you need to memorize to defend arguments about the Second Amendment to have and carry arms.

The number of gun killings dropped 39% between 1993 and 2011, the Bureau of Justice Statistics reported in a separate report. Gun crimes that weren't fatal fell by 69%.

If I went into an average high school classroom or college lecture hall and I asked the students whether gun crime is increasing or decreasing over the past 20 years, my guess is that a majority of them would claim that gun crime is steadily increasing. Why is this?

The answer is very simple. Certain members of the media who want increased gun control, overreport gun crimes consistently to give the illusion that the United States has a massive gun crime problem. Additionally, people remember tragedies more than they do the nightly news. So when people think about gun crime, they automatically think about Sandy Hook, Virginia Tech, and Columbine. Those were terrible tragedies, although even with those calculated into the statistics, we are seeing a massive decrease in overall crime and gun crime.

All of these decreases in crime are occurring despite record-level gun sales. In 2009, FBI background checks for guns increased by 30% over the previous year, while firearms sales increased by almost 40%.

The demand for guns has never been higher in this country, and with more than 300 million guns in circulation, it would seem according to the gun grabbers that crime would be increasing dramatically. But the numbers do not lie.

With more people owning guns today than in any other time in our nation's history and more people practicing concealed carry, it disproves the argument that we need to retract the amount of guns in circulation.

Key Points

- Over the past 20 years, the United States has seen a dramatic decrease in gun crime and overall crime.
- Gun ownership is at an all-time high.
- A majority of Americans believe gun crime is getting worse, when in reality it is consistently improving.
- Public perception does not always reflect reality.

Links

http://articles.latimes.com/2013/may/07/nation/la-na-nn-gun-crimes-pew-report-20130507

http://www.nytimes.com/2013/01/12/us/as-us-weighs-new-rules-sales-of-guns-and-ammunition-surge.html?r=O&_r=0

Myth: Hunters Are Bloodthirsty and Non-Hunters Are Not Able to Enjoy Wildlife

"Even though less than 5% of the U.S. population hunts, non-hunters are forced to share many wildlife refuges, national forests, state parks, and other public lands with armed individuals who enjoy killing animals. Almost 40% of hunters in the U.S. slaughter and maim millions of animals on public land every year. By some estimates, poachers kill just as many animals illegally."

—PETA's website on hunting

To begin the refutation of this myth I have to first draw the bold and important distinction between hunting and poaching. PETA tries to convince people that hunting and poaching are synonymous and involve similar practices. This is a complete falsehood, for hunting is controlled and done in a manner that will preserve the wildlife and leave the habitat better for the next generation. Poachers on the other hand are ruthless criminals who slaughter animals without any regard for the age of the animal or the affect poaching may have on the local wildlife community.

In Africa, poachers work illegally outside government officials to heartlessly deplete the elephant and rhino populations. Hunters, on the other hand, buy their permits legally. They do not kill anymore than they are legally allowed to and invest time, money, and energy into conservation. Poachers have no concern for conserving the land for the next generation, as their objective is to kill as many animals as possible to benefit themselves in the short term.

Hunters across the globe drastically have stepped up their efforts to fight against poaching. Antipoaching efforts are mainly sponsored and paid for by people who regularly hunt. This is because hunters want to do everything possible to preserve the land and the wildlife for future generations.

The International Anti-Poaching Foundation (IAPF) works tirelessly to stop the killing of endangered species across the globe. Founded in 2009 by Damien Mander, an Iraq War veteran who has witnessed massive killings of endangered species across the globe, decided to charter the organization to stand up against these illegal killings.

IAPF raises money and organizes professional conservation experts to go to Africa and begin massive antipoaching efforts. One of the biggest obstacles facing the IAPF is being able to monitor and patrol massive amounts of land. A unique solution the IAPF has invested in is the use of drones to monitor hundreds of square miles. Whenever the antipoachers are able to find poaching occurring, they are much more likely to be able to catch the responsible parties and bring them to justice.

Antipoaching organizations are primarily funded by hunters who have a deep appreciation for seeing the wildlife in Africa and across the globe treated properly. Whenever talking to people who oppose hunting, it is imperative that you differentiate between hunting and poaching. They are two categorically different practices, and hunters should reject any individual who tries to make a comparison between the two.

As stated above, PETA continues a narrative that is pushed by anti-hunters across the country that hunters enjoy the act of killing animals. It alludes to the point that hunters kill animals because they get a pleasure out of the act of killing. In a previous section of this book, I went into great detail about how hunters do not hate animals nor do they derive any pleasure from killing them, so it is important when confronted with that claim to refute it immediately.

The beginning of PETA's statement attacks hunters for hunting on public lands and saying that people are forced to "share" these lands with "armed individuals," as if hunters are going to shoot the tourists. The basis of this claim is that the hunters somehow get special privileges over the hikers and sightseers.

Well, this is just not true, for hunters fund a majority of the parks and conservation through excise taxes on ammunition and licensing fees. The majority of funding for Maryland's state wildlife programs comes from hunting licenses and fees and from a special federal excise tax on sport hunting devices and ammunition. About 90% of Maryland's state budget for wildlife programs comes from these two sources. This is seen across the United States, whereby hunters are the primary funding source of parks and recreational centers.

So to use PETA's own logic against it, let's reword its opening argument: "Only 5% of hunters hunt, but they fund the majority of the lands for the remaining 95% of Americans to enjoy." That makes more sense, doesn't it? PETA is trying to paint that argument against hunters when in reality everyone enjoys the national parks and state parks because of investments hunters have made throughout the years through buying licenses and ammunition.

Key Points

- There is a significant difference between hunting and poaching.
- Most antipoachers are hunters themselves.
- There are many antipoaching groups mobilizing people to take action against illegal killings.
- Wildlife recreational centers are funded almost completely by hunters.
- Hunters do not find a masochistic pleasure in killing animals, unlike what PETA claims.
- Hunters contribute more to wildlife and conservation than any other group.

Myth: Gun Control Does Not Mean Overall Control by the Government

I often hear from professors, friends, and colleagues who truly believe that governmental tyranny and civil unrest is unrealistic and cannot happen in America.

Most of those people I hear this from say that "democracies never go rouge" or "our system of government will prevent us from having massive civil unrest." I think it's extremely important to analyze historical examples of countries that experience governmental tyranny and the steps that took place to get there. If one looks at the history of Nazi Germany and Maoist China you will see that the first step to totalitarian government is unilateral disarmament.

Let's take a look at history over the past 120 years, whereby we will see common trends among countries that disarm their citizenry. A majority of them started with dictators and governments beginning to universally register weapons and then moved to confiscate them in the name of "public safety." Maoist China spent years disarming the public before instituting a reign of terror by killing tens of millions of people and displacing hundreds of millions from their homes and livelihoods.

Shortly after World War I, Germany instituted a gun control policy that made it very restrictive and difficult to access and purchase a gun. Every gun owner was required to have a permit, which was very expensive and hard to come by. When the Nazis took power in 1933 they started house-to-house searches asking for and demanding firearms from the citizens.

They did not just make it illegal to own certain guns and firearms, but they forcibly extracted them from the citizens. They went door to door in an extremely aggressive manner, prying guns away from ordinary people, all in the name of "public safety."

Most of the new laws were anti-Semitic in nature. They prohibited Jews from being in the firearms business, and all guns that were "outside of hunting activities" were made illegal.

Shortly after the confiscation of guns, one of the biggest riots occurred in the Nazi regime—"Kristallnacht," the night of broken glass. Nazi forces raided and plundered Jewish businesses and religious centers.

Just three days after Kristallnacht, Hitler issued an executive order making it illegal for any Jew to own or possess a firearm. This was the beginning of the Holocaust and, by all means, the end of Jewish freedom in Germany. As soon as the Germans had taken away the Jew's right to defend themselves, they stripped the Jews of every other freedom they enjoyed, including the freedom of expression, thought, religious prayer, and even their right to life.

Germany was able to confiscate the weapons easily, for they spent years registering every single gun, with a location and address tied to it. So when it came time to confiscate the guns from the Jews, the Gestapo had a national database of where every single gun was located. It made the confiscation process seamless and disarmament almost too easy.

Another example was in 1956, when Cambodia instituted strict gun control policy and disallowed any citizens from owning guns. Shortly after that, the government killed more than one million defenseless people in cold blood. The people of Cambodia had no way of protecting themselves against a tyrannical government. They were slaughtered by the hundreds of thousands as the government pushed forth its cleansing campaign.

In the Soviet Union, a situation similar to the two examples detailed above occurred. After the Red victory in the civil war, all firearms were made illegal, and if people were found to be in possession of firearms they would be sent to hard labor. In 1925 the law was made even more severe by adding a fine of 300 rubles to the penalty of firearm ownership.

Stalin even went so far as to ban knives in 1935 by making the penalty for ownership of a knife up to five years in prison and even sentencing some individuals to death.

Once Stalin was able to institute his policies to control the population, he began his massive campaign to kill millions of people. In a 10-year span, he killed more than 10 million people, more than all the people who had died in World War I. He was able to successfully execute his massive extermination plan because no citizens were able to resist his tyrannical campaign.

It is very simple—whenever a government confiscates guns and/or puts forth restrictive measures, it is not about guns, but rather it is about control. History is riddled with democracies and countries with governments that go tyrannical. Many people dismiss the notion that governments can go tyrannical and call it a "conspiracy theory." The very simple response to that should be to walk them through history.

The firewall for liberty and freedom in this country is the citizens' ability to defend themselves. In history, when governments act irrational in discriminatory manners, tyranny surely follows.

Imagine our government controlling or eliminating guns and/or ammunition. The government would not have to go too rogue then to install their ideals on a defenseless public. Ever consider who gets medical treatment, or which religion gets banned, or who gets education, or who gets to travel, or who has to work 70 hours per week.

Key Points

- Gun control is not about guns; it's about control.
- Germany made it difficult for Jews to own guns, which made massive extermination easy.
- Soviet Russia, Maoist China, and Nazi Germany combined killed more than 100 million people, and all of their citizenries were disarmed.
- Universal registration makes universal confiscation very simple and easy.
- Having a realistic understanding that government tyranny is a possibility does not make you a conspiracy theorist.

Myth: No One Wants to Take Your Guns Away

"Gun grabber is a mythical boogeyman. No serious person, including
Obama, is even proposing taking away owned guns."
—#StopFearMongering–Toure, February 16, 2013 (via Twitter)

"No one is saying that people's guns should be taken away or that taking the Second Amendment's right away. No one is saying that."
—Don Lemon, CNN, July 22, 2012

"I don't want to change the Second Amendment. I don't want to change
an American's right to bear an arm in their home to defend people. I
want to get rid of these killing machine assault weapons off the street."
—Piers Morgan, January 7, 2013

In efforts to justify further gun control, many big-government advocates
will strike down anyone who makes the claim that "they want to take our guns
away." The media and gun grabbers use this as smokescreen to deflect the main
part of the argument by creating a false sense of certainty that not one person
in Congress or who has power would advocate for gun confiscation.

If we look at recent history and we examine the major gun control push-
ers in the Senate today, we find that many of these members of Congress have
been advocating for massive gun confiscation for years.

In 1995, Senator Diane Feinstein joined *60 Minutes* for an extensive interview on gun control and the policies she wanted to implement in Congress.
Senator Feinstein is the notorious author of the 1994 and the 2013 assault
weapons ban. After the Sandy Hook tragedy, she was the leading voice in

Congress for restrictive gun control measures. Does she want to take our guns away? Let's see what she said in 1995 regarding gun control: "If I could've gotten 51 votes in the Senate of the United States for an outright ban, picking up every one of them—Mr. and Mrs. America, turn 'em all in—I would have done it."

So let's get this straight—according to Toure, Don Lemon, and Piers Morgan, no one wants to take our guns away. But the leading legislator and author of several assault weapon bans said very clearly that if she could've gotten 51 votes, she would have done it. Seems pretty clear that, yes, people do indeed want to take our guns away.

Even further and deeper than that, there is the "slippery slope" argument. Essentially, with every gun measure being passed, piece by piece, eventually gun bans and confiscation will be enacted into public policy.

Many proponents of the Second Amendment and people who have studied the history of Great Britain understand that this belief is not at all far-fetched. Gun control policy takes years, if not decades, to fully implement, and possibly even longer if there is a strong gun culture among the citizens. In Glenn Beck's recent book *Control*, he details the progression toward gun control extremely well when analyzing Great Britain's road to total blanket gun bans.

A history of British gun control:

1689: King William of Orange guarantees his subjects (except Catholics) the right to bear arms for self-defense in a new Bill of Rights.

1819: In response to civil unrest, a temporary Seizure of Arms Act is passed; it allows constables to search for and confiscate arms from people who are "dangerous to the public peace." This act expired after two years.

1870: A license is needed only if you want to carry a firearm outside of your home.

1903: The pistols act is introduced and seems to be full of common sense. No guns for drunks or the mentally insane, and licenses are required for handgun purchases.

1920: The Firearms Act ushers in the first registration system and gives police the power to deny a license to anyone "unfitted to be trusted with a firearm." According to historian Clayton Cramer, this is the true first pivot for the United Kingdom, as "the ownership of firearms ceased to be a right of Englishmen, and instead it became a privilege."

1937: An update to the Firearms Act is passed, which raises the minimum age to buy a gun, gives police more power to regulate licenses, and bans most fully automatic weapons. The home secretary also rules that self-defense is no longer a valid reason to be granted a gun certificate.

1967: The Criminal Justice Act expands licensing to shotguns.

1968: Existing gun laws are placed into a single law. Applicants have to show good reason for carrying ammunition and guns. The home office is also given the power to set fees for shotgun licenses.

1988: After the Hungerford massacre, in which a crazy person uses two semiautomatic rifles to kill 15 people, an amendment to the Firearms Act is passed. According to the BBC, this amendment "banned semi-automatic and pump action rifles; weapons which fire explosive ammunition; short shotguns with magazines; and elevated pump-action and self loading rifles. Registration was also made mandatory for shotguns, which were required to be kept in secure storage."

1997: After the Dunblane massacre results in the death of 16 children and a teacher (the killer uses two pistols and two revolvers"), another Firearms Act is passed, this one essentially banning all handguns.

2006: After a series of gun-related homicides get national attention, the Violent Crime Reduction Act is passed, making it a crime to make or sell imitation guns and further restricting the use of "air weapons."

Piers Morgan, who has said no one wants to take your guns away, made an extremely bold statement on his CNN show on January 10, 2013:

> You've got to make a stand somewhere. You have to start somewhere. The logical place to start, given that automatic weapons are banned, is you go to the next level down, semiautomatic weapons. You know, in an ideal world, I'd have all the guns gone, as we have in Britain. But this is not my country. And I respect the fact that most Americans wouldn't wear that kind of argument.

It seems that Morgan tipped his hand right there and indicated that, yes, he does want to ban all guns. He "wants to start somewhere," and just like his mother country Britain did, when it began down the slope toward total gun bans, it will eventually get there.

If this time line and example detailing British gun control progression does not illustrate the "slippery slope," I am not sure what will. The United Kingdom was once a country with respect for gun ownership, and over a long period of time, it slowly eroded the citizens' right to bear arms. Similar to the Newtown massacre, whenever there is a mass shooting, lawmakers get enormous pressure to put forth stronger and much more strict gun control measures. Although, as I detailed in a previous section of this book, that pressure and support for more gun laws is short-lived and fades out quickly.

Yes, people do want to take your guns away. Reject the argument that "no one is trying to confiscate your guns," for as I have detailed in this section, many legislators and members of the media have been trying for blanket gun bans for years. In addition, do not forget the British example and how piece by piece the British government has chipped away at its citizens' ability to own guns.

Now, let's talk facts. London is one of the most dangerous cities in all of Europe. It has a staggering homicide rate, one of the highest compared to large U.S. cities. It is with knives. The homicide rate from knives has increased to the point that it is dangerous for people to be out at night. Knowing a person is defenseless, an attack with a knife is quick, silent, efficient, and deadly.

Key Points

- There are many members of the media and Congress who vocally support the banning of guns.
- Great Britain is a fantastic example of the slippery slope.
- Senator Feinstein argued in the 1990s for gun confiscation.
- Gun control advocates are very patient and will push measures piece by piece until they accomplish their unilateral gun ban.
- The process of banning guns is a long process, and the people who want to ban them will take every mini victory they can get on the road to complete gun bans.
- Gun control has not worked in London, which has one of the worst homicide rates of all large cities.

Myth: College Students Can't Be Trusted to Carry Guns

"Carrying guns on a college campus, for example, is one of the dumbest things I've ever heard of in my life. I don't remember what you were like when you were in college, but I shouldn't have had a gun when I was in college nor should anybody I knew. We just don't need guns every place."

—Mayor Michael Bloomberg, December 16, 2012

"It's why we have call boxes, it's why we have safe zones, it's why we have the whistles. Because you just don't know who you're going to be shooting at. And you don't know if you feel like you're gonna be raped, or if you feel like someone's been following you or if you feel like you're in trouble and when you might actually not be, that you pop out that gun and you pop-pop a round at somebody?"

—Joe Salazar, Colorado state representative

T his is becoming a hot-button issue as of late—whether college students should be allowed to carry firearms on college campuses for self-protection. The gut reaction for too many people is to immediately say, "Kids cannot be trusted with guns." That may sound like it makes sense, but let's first dive into some data in areas in which conceal carry has been in effect for younger Americans.

In January 2013, five states granted students the right to carry concealed weapons on university campuses: Colorado, Mississippi, Oregon, Utah, and

Wisconsin. Twenty-one states leave that decision up to the individual schools, but most universities that are given the right to decide on their own usually do not allow students the right to carry.

Looking at a few examples in which conceal carry has been allowed on college campuses (Colorado State University since 2003 and Blue Ridge Community College since 1995), for almost 100 combined semesters, none of these schools has seen a single resulting incident of gun violence (even including threats and suicides), a single accident, or a single gun theft.

None of the 40 "right-to-carry" states have seen any sort of resulting increase in gun violence since legalizing concealed carry, despite the fact that licensed citizens regularly carry handguns in public places, such as movie theaters and convenience stores. Many studies done by people such as John Lott, a research scientist from the University of Maryland, and David Mustard, a professor from the University of Georgia, concluded that concealed handgun license holders are up to five times less likely to commit a violent crime versus nonlicense holders.

An emerging movement that has begun to get a lot of traction is the Students for Concealed Carry organization. Comprising more than 43,000 college students from every part of the country, SFCC is made up of students from many viewpoints. It has representation from Democrats, Republicans, Libertarians, Independents, and Anarchists. It functions for two purposes: to dispel myths surrounding gun ownership on college campuses and to push forth policy that will promote responsible gun laws for students on college campuses. SFCC is expanding its reach every day and plans to be able to pass substantive concealed carry policy for students in all 50 states within 10 years.

Upon further examining statistics from a state level, we see that both Florida and Texas have extremely detailed records on the behavior of their permit holders.

Over nearly 25 years, from October 1, 1987, to June 30, 2012, Florida has issued concealed carry permits to nearly 2.4 million people. Very few, only 168, have had those permits revoked for any type of firearms-related violations. The most common reason for revocation had been for carrying the gun in a gun-free zone. Only four permit holders in Florida have had their permits revoked for an actual firearms violation, which amounts to an annual rate of .0001%. Looking at Texas, the numbers are similar. In 2011 there were 519,000 active license holders. Of those, 120 were convicted of either a misdemeanor or a felony in that same year, which is about a rate of 0.023%, and only a few of those crimes involved a gun.

In response to Mr. Salazar's point, gun-free zones don't deter criminals. Criminals and people who break the law will commit crimes regardless of what the signs say. All that gun-free zones do is to prevent law-abiding citizens the right to defend themselves against crime.

On TheBlaze TV, a woman named Amanda Collins had a featured interview with Glenn Beck. Collins was a concealed-carry license holder but was not permitted to carry her gun while on campus. She was brutally raped inside a parking garage less than 100 feet away from campus authorities.

"I was denied the one equalizing factor that I had," she said on TheBlaze. "I was in a safe and gun free zone. My attacker did not care."

Regarding not being able to trust young people with a firearm, I think it is clear that we trust some of our best and brightest to go to war. That it is not a far reach to say we should be able to trust young people with the right to protect themselves domestically. If young adults, 18 and 19 years old, are able to carry M16s and fight for our country, then they should be allowed to protect themselves on a college campus.

Key Points

- States with concealed-carry permits have far less crime among license holders compared to states that do not have concealed weapons permits.
- SFCC is growing and uniting students and showing that concealed carry can save lives and prevent crime.
- Criminals ignore gun-free zones and laws.

Myth: Hunting Is on the Decline

W ith the media continually attacking the Second Amendment and hunting, many people will make it seem that hunting is becoming increasingly unpopular. Anti-hunting groups go to great lengths to give hunting a bad name. In 2009, a feature story on *CBS News* stated that "US Hunting is on the Decline."

It reported: "Hunters remain a powerful force in American society, as evidenced by the presidential candidates who routinely pay them homage, but their ranks are shrinking dramatically and wildlife agencies worry increasingly about the loss of sorely needed license-fee revenue."

New figures from the U.S. Fish and Wildlife Service show that the number of hunters 16 and older declined by 10 percent between 1996 and 2006, from about 14 million to about 12.5 million. The drop was most acute in New England, the Rocky Mountains, and the Pacific states, which lost 400,000 hunters in that span.

The article did not say anything factually incorrect. In fact, it is true. Until 2006 the number of hunters in the United States was declining. But here is the biggest problem with this article—it was written in 2009 and is still being touted by many anti-hunting groups as a key piece of evidence that hunting is on the decline. Since that article was written, we have seen drastic changes in the numbers of new hunters beginning to take up the sport, as well as the emergence of a new type of hunter that sometimes cannot be shown in the U.S. Fish and Wildlife's statistics.

Near the end of 2011, the head of the Department of Interior, Ken Salazar, announced a report with new findings regarding hunting. His department, after doing extensive research and collaboration with state and local agencies, reported that they found that the number of hunters had increased by 9% over the past five years.

Salazar called the new findings of the outdoor research survey "outstanding news."

Many state parks are beginning to see their revenues increase dramatically because of the increase in hunters. In just 2011 alone, 13.7 million people hunted and spent more than 34 billion dollars on equipment, licenses, and other items, which amounts to more than 2,484 dollars per hunter.

When hunting numbers go up, conservation efforts also improve.

"Hunters and anglers are the key funders of fish and wildlife conservation through their license and gear purchases," said Jonathan Gassett, commissioner of the Kentucky Fish and Wildlife Resources Commission and president of the Association of Fish and Wildlife Agencies. "An increase in participation and expenditure rates means that agencies can continue to restore and improve habitat for fish and wildlife species, bring more youth into the outdoors and provide even greater access to recreational activities."

As we begin to see the increase in hunting, we have to reexamine the way we do hunting surveys and how we categorize people as "hunters." For example, a study done by the National Shooting Sports Foundation (NSSF) found that over the past five years, more than 21.8 million people hunted at least once, and they came to the same conclusion that the Department of Interior came to—that 14 million people regularly hunt each year.

But the NSSF argued in its study that to accurately tell how much of the general population hunts, we must start looking at an emerging trend called "casual hunting." This category comprises people and families who enjoy the sport of hunting but might not be in a desirable geographic location to hunt or might have newfound financial constraints that limit them from hunting on a regular basis.

Further examination by the NSSF shows that, when looking at purchasing patterns over multiple years, for every two hunters in the field this year, at least one is taking a year off.

Massive urbanization is making it difficult for some people to get out into the field every year. It is hard during postrecessionary times to be able to afford to pay for hunts, but that does not mean that hunting as a whole is on the decline; it just means that hunters are going about the sport more differently than ever before.

Many of these casual hunters do not purchase hunting licenses, nor do they participate in regular donations to hunting organizations. Many surveys look just at hunting license growth for determining the number of hunters in a society over a period of time. But the NSSF study shows us that those who fall into the emerging causal hunting demographic (more than seven million people) are unlikely to buy hunting licenses regularly but will continue to support hunting throughout their lifetimes.

Key Points

- Up until 2006, hunting was on the decline.
- New numbers show that hunting is up almost 9% in 2011 since 2006.
- State parks rely on hunters buying hunting licenses for their revenue.
- "Casual hunters" is a growing demographic of people who hunt but do not hunt every year.
- The country was in a recession from approximately 2008 to 2010, perhaps into 2011, as business was poor and unemployment high. Yet in that poor economic environment many people hunted and paid for the cost of their sport.

Myth: The NRA Has Blood on Its Hands

"The NRA is killing our kids."

—Medea Benjamin, codirector of Code Pink

T he NRA has become the poster child for almost all gun-related tragedies in the past decade. Members of the media, anti-gun advocates, and a good chunk of teachers blame the NRA for the supposed "escalation" of gun violence in the United States. As I detailed in a previous chapter, gun violence has actually gone down dramatically over the past 20 years, contrary to what many Americans think. Despite the empirical data that show gun violence is indeed decreasing, the media need to pin the blame on some entity whenever there is a massive gun massacre.

After Sandy Hook, the NRA was front-page news for almost three continuous weeks. Executive vice president of the NRA, Wayne LaPierre, testified in front of Congress for the first time in nearly a decade. Piers Morgan, along with many other members of the media, led an all-out attack against the NRA. Before we jump to any conclusions as to whether the NRA is to blame for massive shootings or gun violence, let's first establish why the NRA was founded, the initiatives it is involved in, and the actual policy prescriptions it has to gun violence.

In 1871 Union veterans Colonel William C. Church and General George Wingate formed the National Rifle Association. The main goal of the organization was to "promote and encourage rifle shooting on a scientific basis."

Both Church and Wingate founded the NRA because they were dismayed at the lack of marksmanship that was being exhibited by their own troops.

After 30 years of successfully promoting marksmanship and responsible gun ownership, the NRA began shooting sport initiatives for youths on major colleges, universities, and military academies across the country. By 1906 NRA's youth program was in full operation, with more than 200 boys competing in shooting matches that summer. To date, the youth training program is still a cornerstone of the core of the NRA's mission. Each year one million youths participate in NRA shooting sports events, which also foster safe and responsible gun ownership.

For the next 40 years the NRA continued being the leading voice for responsible gun ownership and understanding the importance of the Second Amendment. In the 1930s the NRA founded its legislative arm (NRA-ILA), which is still in full operation today and advocates for legislation and policy that will promote the Second Amendment and protect the rights of responsible gun owners.

The NRA diversified its reach in the 1930s with a large push to recruit hunters to join the NRA. In its push, the NRA included an agenda to institute a massive conservation education program that included specific measures to help preserve and protect wildlife for the next generation.

The NRA supported the Pittman-Robertson Act of 1937, which promoted an excise tax on ammunition and guns to help pay for additional conservation projects in the southeast region.

During the continued spread of the NRA, the civil rights movement was heating up in the 1960s. The NRA began helping to set up charters to train local African American communities to protect and defend themselves. In Monroe, North Carolina, in 1960, the NRA, in conjunction with the NAACP, trained local citizens on how to use guns to defend themselves against the Ku Klux Klan. One night a citizen successfully defended an assault by the KKK on one of the NAACP leader's homes without any casualties.

As the NRA continued to expand, up until the 1990s, its reach to our nation's youth was unparalleled. The NRA invested significant money, time, and energy into firearms instruction, which today has more than 55,000 certified instructors, with more than 750,000 people trained each year.

The Eddie Eagle GunSafe program, sponsored by the NRA, has been extremely successful. The program uses young children's vocabulary and outreach methods to teach children that "if you find a gun, stop, don't touch, leave the area, tell an adult." The message has reached more than 25 million kids since its inception in 1988.

One of the biggest critiques of the NRA is that "it is funded through gun corporations and special interests," although, according to FactCheck.org, nearly half of the funding for the NRA comes from membership dues alone. Voluntary donations to the NRA still account for a majority of the remaining funding, which includes voluntary donations made during gun purchases, as well as during the "round up for the NRA" campaign.

Essentially, the campaign is an operation sponsored by retailers whereby customers can "round up" their purchases to the nearest dollar and donate the proceeds to the NRA. Yes, gun companies do donate to the NRA, just like drug companies donate to drug lobbies and defense companies donate to defense lobbies.

The NRA is the leading voice for gun ownership in the United States, and despite the myths, it is majorly funded by grassroots donations.

The NRA's current stance on gun control is very simple: to enforce the existing laws more aggressively and in a better fashion. In 2008, after the Virginia Tech shooting, the NRA helped pass the NICS Improvement Act. The bill increases funding and grants to states to report vital information to the National Instant Criminal Background Check System. The NRA also advocated for increased prosecution for those who lie on their background checks when purchasing firearms.

The NRA is not against gun laws; instead it is against new, irrational laws that are not written using substantive policy and are instead trying to politicize a massacre for advancement of a certain political agenda.

After learning that the NRA spends millions of dollars each year teaching young people about the Second Amendment and gun safety, it is easy to conclude that the intention of the NRA is not as Ms. Benjamin from Code Pink said: "The NRA is killing our kids." Those sorts of irrational, short-sighted comments should be rejected and dismissed by the media.

But instead, after she snuck into a press conference with Wayne LaPierre of the NRA, she stood up with a huge sign that read "The NRA has blood on its hands." That very same night, Piers Morgan had her on for a feature interview. Not only do the media buy into this narrative; they promote it on prime-time television.

Additionally, a common talking point spread about the NRA is that it "buys off politicians" and because of this "nothing gets done."

> I have been stunned by the sheer political cowardice of so many politicians in America who seem just terrified of saying anything that the NRA may object towards. The NRA has four million members. America has 310 million people living here. I just don't understand why everybody is so cowardly about publicly dealing with this and trying to get the exact measures that you've [Connecticut Senator Richard Blumenthal] just suggested.
>
> —Piers Morgan, December 20, 2012

Very simply, there are many other organizations that engage in lobbying outside of the NRA. According to OpenSecrets.org the NRA is not even in the top 10 of the biggest lobbying groups in the country. Huge corporate lobbying budgets dwarf the NRA's footprint of legislative influence. The AARP spends almost twice as much annually as the NRA does on lobbying. The media do not seem to have a problem with the AARP spending millions on campaigns and lobbying efforts, but why do they consistently target the NRA for "buying politicians"?

Another contention Morgan made is that the NRA "only" has four million members. To give some perspective, other membership-based groups, such as the ACLU, have about 500,000 members. But supporters of the Second Amendment are not limited to just NRA members. It is extremely important to make the distinction that there are millions of people who hunt, own guns, and support the Second Amendment but who are not part of the NRA.

It comes down to a deeper, more fundamental issue than lobbying and membership. It comes down to the representation of the people and how they view gun ownership and the NRA. If a large majority of Americans favored increased gun control, they would make it a point to remove elected officials who take money from the NRA and push forth that sort of gun control.

A very interesting Gallup poll has been conducted since 1959 and shows American's feelings on gun control. The question posed is: Do you think there should be a law banning the possession of handguns, except by the police and other authorized persons? Following are the results of the people who answered "Yes, there should be":

- 1959: 60%
- 1965: 49%
- 1975: 41%
- 1988: 37%
- 1999: 34%
- 2006: 32%
- 2009: 28%
- 2012: 24%

This drastic change in public opinion shows that people are increasingly comfortable with the idea of gun ownership.

A similar poll, also conducted by Gallup (because of the assault weapons ban being pushed in the 1990s, this poll started in 1996), asked the question, Should it be illegal to manufacture, sell, or possess semiautomatic guns known as assault rifles? The results follow:

- 1996: 57% in support
- 2004: 50% in support
- 2012: 44% in support

The anti-gun advocates, such as Morgan, need to realize that it is not the NRA that is out of touch with the American people; it is the anti-gun agenda that is contrary to what the American people think.

Members of the NRA include Democrats, Republicans, Independents, Liberals, and Conservatives.

The NRA is not a "right-wing attack dog," as some media personalities portray it as being. Instead, the NRA is a manifestation of individuals coming together who believe in the right to bear arms.

Every NRA member might have a different reason he or she wants to bear arms. Some might want to engage in competitive shooting, others might want to defend their homes or businesses, and still others might want to pass down an old family-owned firearm.

But what is important to remember is that NRA is one of the oldest civil rights organizations in the history of this country and that for a century and a half the NRA has stood strong and continually helped defend the inalienable right to bear arms.

Key Points

- The NRA was founded in 1871 and remains a grass root funded organization.

- Americans might be surprised to know that in 1960 the NRA and the NAACP joined forces to fight the Ku Klux Klan with the NRA teaching Afro Americans about guns and how to use them.

- For many years the NRA has spent millions of dollars each year teaching kids about gun safety and providing gun safety courses.

- It is interesting to be aware that AARP spends almost twice as much money lobbying politicians as does the NRA, a fact not brought out in the news media.

- In 1959 60% of the people thought there should be a law banning possession of handguns, but in 2012 that percentage dropped to 24%.

- In 1996 57% of the people believed it should be illegal to manufacture, sell, or possess semi automatic guns known as assault rifles, but in 2012 that percentage dropped to 44%.

- The NRA is one of the strongest organizations in America fighting to protect our right to bear arms.

- Remember, let a government take away one right from a citizen, another right will be lost soon after.

Myth: Militia Means Only a Few People of a Force

The Second Amendment states: "A well regulated Militia, being necessary to the security of a free State, the right of the people to keep and bear Arms, shall not be infringed."

But what does a well-regulated militia mean? Does it mean that the Second Amendment pertains only to people who are in the national guard or police force?

Many anti-gun control advocates argue in favor of more control by saying "militia means only a select few people who are part of an organized force."

The Daily Kos posted on December 25, 2012: "Until this so-called militia is being adequately regulated, the purported right of the people to keep and bear arms MUST be infringed. If it is not regulated (or infringed upon), such a militia actually undermines and threatens the security of the state."

Let's look back to when the founders were writing the Constitution and analyze what a militia was back then. During the times of the founders, every town had a militia, but it may be different than what you think, for a militia was made up of every able-bodied man in the village. It was not a selective service; instead it was everyone who owned a gun and was able to walk. Despite what many gun control advocates will tell you, a militia just means a group of everyday individuals.

Daily Kos continued by saying, "The best case for gun control was made in the Second Amendment. After all, it says they [guns] should be regulated."

I think it's important that we first define what "regulated" meant back when the founders wrote the Constitution. "Well regulated" meant "well trained, prepared, and disciplined." Some seem to think that "regulated militia" means only the state's national guard. But looking at what the founders wrote in the Federalist Papers, the intent of a "militia" was to give individual citizens the right to bear arms and protect themselves.

The Oxford dictionary during that time defined "regulated" as being something that was "well calibrated and functioning as expected." That is a much different definition than the modern view of the word "regulated."

The current definition is, "Control or supervise (something, esp. a company or business activity) by means of rules and regulations," a much different definition than the one put forth by the founders. It is important whenever analyzing documents written by the founders that we look at the intent of the writings and also whether the words they chose have the same weight and meaning today.

James Madison, the author of the Bill of Rights, wrote: "The ultimate authority resides in the people, and if the federal government got too powerful and overstepped its authority then the people would develop plans of resistance and resort to arms" (Federalist Paper number 46).

Madison makes it clear in his elaboration of the Second Amendment that it is not just for governmental people to possess arms or militias but rather "the people." As I elaborated earlier in this book, the fundamental purpose of the Second Amendment is not self-defense but instead to be able to resist government tyranny. It gives the people the ability to protect their freedoms and liberties.

The founders intentionally designed it as a way for the citizens to stand up to the government. Therefore, it is not consistent to argue that only the government should possess firearms when respecting the intent of the founders.

Key Points

- James Madison, the author of the Bill of Rights, wrote: "The ultimate authority resides in the people, and that if the federal government go too powerful and overstepped its authority, then the people would develop plans of resistance and resort to arms." It is plain and obvious what our founding fathers wanted our country to be when we became a country. They wanted a country of the people and not a country of the government.

Myth: Assault Weapons Are Responsible for More Crime

As we look deeper into the history of the term "assault weapon," we will realize it is a completely made-up term that has been perpetuated and advanced for the passage of a political agenda. According to a study in the *Stanford Law and Policy Review*, done by Kobayashi and Olson: "Prior to 1989 the term 'assault weapon' did not exist in the lexicon of firearms. It is a political term, developed by anti-gun publicists to expand the category of 'assault rifles' so as to allow an attack on as many additional firearms as possible on the basis of undefined 'evil appearance.'"

Ask any responsible gun owner to define what an assault weapon is, and she or he will have little idea of what you are talking about. Anti-gun legislators have coined and owned the term for almost two decades now as a way to push forth legislation that will remove many guns from the marketplace.

In 1994 Senator Diane Feinstein was successful in passing a bill in the Senate that banned the sale of certain weapons. She used the political term "assault weapon." After the Sandy Hook tragedy, she used the attention that was drawn to guns to try to reintroduce her weapons ban that was first implemented back in 1994 and then expired in 2004.

Luckily, we have very convincing data that the ban Senator Feinstein helped institute was indeed a failure. A report conducted by the Department of Justice claims in regard to the assault weapons ban that "it failed to reduce the average number of victims per gun murder incident of multiple gunshot wound victims." The report continued to say that "there was no discernible reduction in the lethality and injuriousness of gun violence."

So we know that the bill did not work; in fact, it failed miserably. But what exactly would the bill have banned and what did its authors hope to achieve? Examining the intricacies of the bill we find that the proposal that was put forth and pushed by Senator Feinstein would have simply banned certain cosmetic features of a firearm. Senator Feinstein's bill would have banned guns that looked scary by banning pistol grips, folding rifle stocks, threaded barrels for attaching silencers, and guns that had the ability to accept ammunition magazines holding large numbers of bullets.

Her attempt to curb gun violence and bring down gun crime was not an attack on the actual functionality of any firearms; instead it was aiming to ban things that looked like they should be illegal.

Senator Ted Cruz from Texas articulated this masterfully in a joint committee hearing on gun violence when reintroduction of Senator Feinstein's bill was being discussed. In the hearing, he put up a picture of a Remington rifle and said, "Under the current bill, this gun would be perfectly legal. Although, if I put this piece of plastic stock (he then held up a plastic pistol grip) up the rifle it immediately becomes illegal."

Senator Cruz ended the hearing by stating that "none of your provisions change the performance characteristics of these firearms." Senator Cruz is exactly right—the assault weapons ban does not address the actual functionality or processing for firearms.

Even if Senator Feinstein had a legitimate point in banning these weapons for how scary they look, the facts prior to the passage of her ban in 1994 do not back up why she would be passing the bill to deter gun violence.

Studies show that, leading up to the passage of her 1994 assault weapons ban, only 1% to 6% of all gun crimes committed were done so using guns that were assault weapons deemed "illegal." A Department of Justice report stated, "The relative rarity of assault weapons used in crime can be attributed to a number of factors. They are long guns, which are used in crime much less often than handguns, and are more expensive and more difficult to conceal than the types of handguns that are used most frequently in crime."

Looking closer at crime rates from the FBI we find that just targeting assault rifles to deter crime is not where the majority of crime in the United States occurs. Following are statistics from the FBI crime report for murder in 2011:

- 323 were committed with rifles
- 496 were committed with hammers and clubs
- 1,694 were committed with knives

The assault weapons ban is a purely political agenda; it is not for the safety of kids and grandkids. The entire argument is built on smeared statistics and an agenda trying to ban guns that look scary. It also stems from the belief that whenever there is a tragedy, massive governmental action is needed to prevent such a thing from happening again. Senator Cruz stated this perfectly when he said, "Sometimes this body [the Senate] acts on emotion and not on facts. And too often that results in bad policy."

Whenever you get into a debate regarding assault weapons, immediately reject the term "assault weapon" because many people who push for anti-gun legislation do not understand what an assault weapon is. They believe those guns should be banned because they look scary and seem to pose a threat to the security of others. But do not be afraid to stand strong and articulate that "assault weapons" are no more deadly than the most innocent-looking gun.

Key Points

- Assault weapon was never a term before 1989. It was a political term expanding the term assault rifle.
- A report by the Department of Justice proved the temporary ban on assault weapons did not reduce the average number of victims per gun murder incident of multiple gunshot wound victims and that there was no discernible reduction in the lethality and injuriousness of gun violence.
- In 1911 the FBI reported only 323 murders with rifles compared to 2,190 committed with hammers, clubs, and knives.

Myth: Boy Scouts Are Just a School Exercise

Nothing could be worse than such an assumption.

The Boy Scout program includes considerable outdoor activity. Boy Scouts play a big role in educating young people about hunting, guns, and conservation.

One of the most interesting programs is that of the Ranger Award Medal of the Boy Scouts for hunting. Requirements for this award are as follows:

1. a. Successfully complete the hunter education course offered by your state wildlife conservation agency.

   b. Learn and explain the requirements to become a volunteer hunter education instructor in your state.

   c. Explain how to report a wildlife-related violation to the appropriate law enforcement agency.

2. Do a, b, or c.

   a. Successfully complete a bow hunter education course offered by your state for the National Bow Hunter Education Foundation.

   b. Successfully complete a National Muzzle Loading Rifle Association basic course.

   c. Participate in a National Rifle Association international Hunter Education Association Youth Hunter Educational Challenge event sponsored by your state.

3. Do a, b, or c.

   a. Assist a certified hunter education instructor with a hunter education course. Review the ETHIC (Educational Tools for Hunters:

Improving Choices) materials provided by Tread Lightly! and the Specialty Vehicle Institute of America to see how they can be used in the course.
   b. Either plan or assist in putting on a National Hunting and Fishing Day program.
   c. Talk with a game warden/conservation officer about his/her job. If possible, observe/assist a game check station in your state.
4. Plan and carry out a hunting trip approved by an adviser.
5. Make a tabletop display or presentation on what you have learned for your crew, another crew, a Cub or Boy Scout group, or another youth group.

I am an Eagle Scout and can proudly say that the Boy Scouts has taught me the importance of nature and conservation. In fact, my first experience of shooting a gun was through the Boy Scouts. It's taught me not only how to shoot a gun but also taught me about gun safety and the importance of how conservation and hunting worked hand in hand.

A friend of mine, Bill Montgomery, who became an Eagle Scout in 1956, told me about his experiences as a camp counselor at the Boy Scout Camp Wokanda in Peoria, Illinois. His primary responsibility was to teach nature to the Boy Scout campers. It was there that he learned how important the balance of humans and nature is.

He told me that it was the Boy Scouts that had taught him how to shoot a gun and a bow and arrow. More importantly, it taught him how the Indians in the valley of that camp had hunted to feed their families. He said that it was in the summer of 1956 that he realized just how important hunting and conservation were.

Boy Scouts have been doing conservation projects for more than 100 years. Among the many projects has been to plant shrubs, trees, and ground cover to help prevent soil erosion. Scouts know that to protect wildlife they must help, which is why so many Scouts become hunters and understand that hunting is good for conservation of wildlife.

The Boy Scouts has played a major role in teaching boys about shooting and gun safety since its beginnings in 1910. Liz Merrell, development director, Utah National Parks Council, said, "Most firearm accidents are due to curiosity and lack of knowledge. Preventing injuries can be as simple as encouraging boys to shoot under the Boy Scout merit badge program."

In my opinion, the Boy Scouts has done more for conservation and gun safety through its educational programs than any other youth organization. The Boy Scouts has also shown how hunting has in the past played an important role in feeding families and maintaining a balance in nature.

Key Points

- The Boy Scouts' program includes a wide variety of activities which includes summer camps and various classes of outdoor activities including educating young people about hunting, guns, and conservation.

Myth: Hunters Do Nothing for Conservation

In the early 1900s, hunters across the United States began to notice a sharp decline in the whitetail deer populations. Fathers and sons who used to go deer hunting would struggle to even see a single deer on their hunts. One hunter from 1922 recalled, "I remember walking through the forest for hours on end and not even seeing one whitetail. It was as if they all disappeared."

Collectively, the hunting community rose as one and took a stand against unregulated hunting and poaching that were being practiced by criminally minded people across the United States.

The problem got so bad that by 1930 experts hypothesized that there were about only 300,000 deer left in North America. With that knowledge hunters began to donate massive tracts of land all over the plains to begin to raise and conserve the deer population. Anti-poaching efforts were also accelerated, and hunters began to push for conservation laws in the sphere of public policy.

Hunters would start localized community-based groups to go out into the local forests and track down and arrest poachers. They then began to establish safe zones, in which deer could graze freely and reproduce. For decades on end, the community took the problem by its horns and started rebuilding a vastly decimated deer population.

During the rise of the conservation movement, hunters "put on themselves" a tax on all firearms, ammunition, and archery equipment. The taxes went to help fund restoration efforts, wildlife research, and animal protection. The Pittman-Robertson excise tax has been in effect since 1937 and is still in effect today, generating more than half a billion dollars annually for conservation.

It is important to remember that hunters were the ones who took a stand against the massive killing of whitetail deer. Hunters knew the land, knew the game, and knew the species, and they organized the efforts to save the very game they loved. Similar to the Ducks Unlimited efforts, hunters have contributed the most to saving wildlife and animals.

Today, because of the efforts of hunters in the early 1900s, there are now more than 30 million whitetail deer in North America.

Deer hunting funds most of the wildlife conservation in many states and is a key source of revenue for many local economies. By comparison, non-hunters and anti-gun people do little for conservation.

What would have happened to whitetail deer if there had been no hunters? The answer is simple: the slaughter and poaching of these animals would have continued. We are able today to enjoy deer as a result of the selfless sacrifice of hunters.

Non-hunters and anti-gun people generally do very little for conservation. get nothing but a blank stare. This is in sharp contrast to what the hunting community does for land and wildlife conservation. Hunters want their kids to hunt. They know that if they do not practice conservation, their kids will have nothing to hunt.

Most hunters will point out that the majority of non-hunters and anti-hunters contribute the majority of their funds to fight hunters and gun control, but little or no money is invested constructively for wildlife, nature or state facilities.

It is the money from hunting licenses that pays for state parks, which non-hunters seldom even pay a dime to use. It is also license money that pays for game and fish personnel who manage our wildlife.

The stories go on and on. For example, "Hunting Is Conservation" is the motto of one of the most successful and storied conservation groups in the country—the Rocky Mountain Elk Foundation (RMEF). It was founded in 1984 by four hunters from Montana who realized that there were many other groups doing fantastic work in the realm of conserving turkey, duck, and moose but that little was being done to protect and preserve elk.

Through years of hard work and fund-raising, the RMEF was able to garner support from hunters across the region. Countless hunters donated tracts of land, plus spent time and money to help the cause. Today, the Rocky Mountain Elk Foundation has more than 6.5 million acres of land dedicated to nothing but conservation.

The Foundation serves elk by establishing migration corridors and calving grounds, while focusing on securing and improving hunter access throughout elk country. By setting up a system of land donations, RMEF has been able to set up breeding areas and safe zones for elk to live and multiply.

In the early 1900s, as the American conservation movement began to build, hunters began to also notice a sharp decline in the North American turkey populations. Turkeys had become victims of terrible habitat destruction and commercial harvest. Near the end of the 1920s fewer than 30,000 turkeys remained in the entire United States.

Prompted by their love of the animal and nature, hunters began to band together to foster safe places in which turkeys could live and grow in peace. Hunters began implementing propelled nets, which allowed wildlife managers to safely trap wild turkeys and move them to areas with suitable habitats. Conservation-minded outdoorsmen spent millions of dollars and donated countless acres of land to help supplement the cause of preserving turkeys and fostering their multiplication.

In 1973 the National Wildlife Turkey Foundation was created to help supplement the growth and rise of turkey hunting in the United States. In 1973 only 22 states had turkey hunting seasons. Today, there are hunting seasons in 49 states, as well as in Canada and Mexico. Back in the early 1900s it was estimated that there were about 30,000 wild turkeys, and now there are more than seven million in the United States—an amazing testament to conservation and the "true heart" of a hunter.

At its core, hunting truly is conservation. We have shown examples of how hunters have saved ducks from near extinction in North America throughout the 1920s and 1930s. We have looked at whitetail deer and have seen how hunters banded together to collectively agree that the deer needed to be saved and preserved.

Hunters are always thinking about the next generation, whether it be about preserving hunting land so it will be better for their children or teaching their sons and daughters the small nuances of hunting. Hunters are consistently preserving and conserving for the next generation. The heart and soul of a hunter lies in the land, the game, and the nature of the hunt.

Hunters lay down their lives. They donate their time, money, and resources to ensure that their children and grandchildren can enjoy the same experiences they have had. Hunters are truly unique in this manner, and without their steadfast efforts, we would not be able to enjoy turkey, elk, moose, ducks, and many other of our favorite members of wildlife.

A longtime hunter told me that sport hunting is an individual challenge! You are competing with nature, and you, the hunter, are at a disadvantage.

For example,

If you are hunting whitetail deer, you are in their domain.

If you wear smelly clothing, you are done.

If you make a noise, you are done.

If you approach downwind, you are done.

If your gear does not perform, you are done.

If your rifle is not accurate, you are done.

If you're nervous when you shoot, you are done.

If you use a call incorrectly, you are done.

If the weather turns bad, you are done.

There are so many variables! That is why hunters do not harvest a deer every year. You must remember, hunting is a personal challenge in the boxing ring of nature.

That longtime hunter said it so well: "Only those determined are usually successful, a personal achievement."

Key Points

- More people should know and understand what some key hunting conservation groups do for conservation . . . such as Ducks Unlimited, the Rocky Mountain Elk Foundation, the National Wildlife Turkey Foundation, and hundreds of others whose money goes to conservation and who are not out bragging about what they do. It is unfortunate the voices of the true conservationists in this country are not heard.

- Hunters encouraged Fish and Game Departments of all states to write fair laws and regulations to protect numbers and development of wildlife.

Summary: A Call to Action: Courage in the Classroom

This book was written for a reason. I wrote it to ensure that every single young person who reads it will be able to defend and understand the truth behind the Second Amendment and hunting. Too often in our schools and lecture halls we allow anti-gun rhetoric to seep into our curriculum and classrooms. It is not always the fault of teachers, for there are many myths that continue to be spread by people about the Second Amendment. The problem is that they are misinformed or have been taught falsehoods throughout their lives.

If you believe in the Second Amendment and hunting, you have an obligation to stand up and fight for the principles of responsible gun ownership and the right to bear arms. The narrative is owned and controlled by the anti-gun advocates and big-government proponents. This will never change until every hunter, gun owner, and individual who believes in and loves this country stands proudly to not allow our youth to be ridiculed or bullied for their beliefs.

I have been ridiculed and ostracized for my belief by teachers and students. I know how hard it is to challenge teachers or professors. They will use methods of intimidation to suppress the free flow of information and ideas.

Unfortunately, too many teachers use their platform as authority figures to advance an agenda. Classrooms are supposed to be places of learning and discovery, not for intimidation and indoctrination.

Proper debate and disagreement are necessary for a healthy classroom environment. Remember, when you debate and challenge these ideas it is not the teachers who you are trying to change but rather the students around you who will be watching the clash of ideas. Never fear to confront these false ideals head on.

This book has supplied you with the proper intellectual ammunition to fire back. It is time to rise out of the foxhole and fight back with every fact and statistic, story and example that has been provided to you. Rise and defend the ideals that millions have fought and died for before you. You are not alone. Millions across the country go through ridicule every day for believing in the Second Amendment. The time has come to collectively band together and push back against the big-government aggression that has controlled the narrative for the past 50 years. Seize the opportunity—fire back.

Charlie Kirk
Founder of Turning Point USA
turningpointusa.net